THE EAST-WEST CENTER, established in Hawaii by the United States Congress in 1960, is a national educational institution with multinational programs. Its purpose is to promote better relations and understanding among the nations and peoples of Asia, the Pacific area, and the United States through their cooperative participation in research, study, and training activities.

Fundamental to the achievement of the Center's purpose are the cooperative discovery and application of knowledge and the interchange of knowledge, information, ideas, and beliefs in an intercultural atmosphere of academic freedom. In Center programs, theory and practice are combined to help current and future leaders generate, test, and share knowledge about important world problems of mutual concern to people in both East and West.

Each year about 1,500 scholars, leaders, public officials, mid-level and upper-level managers, and graduate students come to the Center to work and study together in programs concerned with seeking alternative approaches and solutions to common problems. For each participant from the United States, two come from the Asian/Pacific area. An international, interdisciplinary professional staff provides the framework, content, and continuity for programs and for cooperative relationships with universities and other institutions in the Center's area of operations.

Center programs are conducted by the East-West Communication Institute, the East-West Culture Learning Institute, the East-West Food Institute, the East-West Population Institute, and the East-West Technology and Development Institute. Each year the Center also awards a limited number of "Open Grants" for graduate degree education and researched by scholars and authorities in areas not encompassed by the problem-oriented institutes.

The East-West Center is governed by the autonomous board of a public, nonprofit educational corporation—the Center for Cultural and Technical Interchange Between East and West, Inc.—established by special act of the Hawaii State Legislature. The Board of Governors is composed of distinguished individuals from the United States and countries of Asia and the Pacific area. The United States Congress provides basic funding for Center programs and for a variety of scholarships, fellowships, internships, and other awards. Because of the cooperative nature of Center programs, financial support and cost-sharing arrangements also are provided by Asian and Pacific governments, regional agencies, private enterprise, and foundations.

The Center is located in Honolulu, Hawaii, on twenty-one acres of land adjacent to the University of Hawaii's Manoa campus. Through cooperative arrangements with the University of Hawaii, the Center has access to University degree programs, libraries, computer center, and the like.

East-West Center Books are published by The University Press of Hawaii to further the Center's aims and programs.

Strategies
for Human Settlements:
Habitat and Environment

Strategies for Human Settlements: *Habitat and Environment*

edited by Gwen Bell

𞥊 An East-West Center Book

from the East-West Technology and Development Institute

The University Press of Hawaii
Honolulu

Manufactured in the United States of America
Designed by Dave Comstock
Composition by Asco Trade Typesetting Limited, Hong Kong

Library of Congress Cataloging in Publication Data

Main entry under title:

Strategies for human settlements: habitat and environment

"An East-West Center book from the East-West
Technology and Development Institute."
1. Cities and towns—Addresses, essays, lectures.
2. Community development—Addresses, essays, lectures.   3. Technology and civilization—Addresses,
essays, lectures.   4. Environmental policy—Addresses, essays, lectures.   I. Bell, Gwen, 1934–
HT65.S77   301.36   76-5416
ISBN 0-8248-0414-7
ISBN 0-8248-0469-4 pbk.

Contents

Foreword

The Technology and Development Institute (TDI) of the East-West Center in Hawaii is pleased to collaborate with the United Nations Environment Program (UNEP) in the publication of this volume.

This collection represents a timely and most unusual contribution to the identification of, and proposed solutions for problems, and to methods for improving the quality of life in human settlements throughout the world. The contributing authors are recognized experts in fields of direct concern in human settlements, including adequate shelter, public health measures (safe water-supply systems and sanitation), food, energy, transportation, communications, and a workable system for better management of natural resources. The papers represent an effort to pull together a comprehensive cross-section of problems and innovative solutions to provide valuable insights and strategies for solving many of these problems in different socioeconomic and climatic environments. The strategies should be of value to all persons interested in human habitation, such as planners, designers, public officials concerned with habitation in its broadest aspects, policymakers, and academicians.

TDI's primary interest in collaborating in such a publication is to project its own substantive emphasis on the role of technology in promoting development. Its program mandate, as one or the East-West Center's problem-oriented institutes, is to seek understanding and better relations between East and West through cooperative generation and application of knowledge about technologically oriented aspects of social and economic development. Accordingly, the institute focuses attention, through its research, professional development and graduate studies programs, on the fourfold problems of employment-oriented development planning, technological adaptation, entrepreneurship development, and public policy and institutional development. In this context, the institute is concerned with social, economic, cultural, and political factors which affect development and the adoption of new ideas. Its focus is on the adaptation, innovation, and diffusion of technologies appropriate to the development situation of each national society.

One of the institute's major activities relevant to technological adaptation is concerned with low-cost housing technology. Cooperative research and development efforts among a number of Asian and American institutions have been ongoing with major substantive and coordinative participation on the part of TDI. The effort in housing technology is intimately related to the other three problem areas and is based on the premise that innovations here must satisfy a number of economic and sociological factors. Among these are:

1. Reduction of the cost of an acceptable housing unit.
2. Creation of a significant number of new jobs through the net effect of technological innovations on the combined building-material and construction industries.
3. Consideration of the attitudes of the people concerned, so that the final product is both useful and usable.
4. Provision of low-cost water supply and waste-disposal systems for public health-control measures.

The solutions will require interdisciplinary action among architects, economists, engineers, and social scientists to provide the necessary framework for analyzing all the problems inherent in applying low-cost housing technology to different socio-economic environments. Ultimately, the total spectrum of the problems of human settlements will be addressed, ranging from research on and development of building materials and designs to methodology of physical planning, social and functional aspects of low-cost housing, and developing a viable indigenous building-industry base.

The institute's cooperative project in low-cost housing technology is described in Part III of this book.

Manuel S. Alba, *Director*
Louis J. Goodman, *Assistant Director*
Albert Dietz, *Senior Fellow*

Preface

ERIC CARLSON ★

We are at the threshold of a new era of international understanding and action for improved habitat and human settlements.
Settlements will be viewed increasingly as ecosystems composed
of natural and man-made elements that interact in complex ways
within the dynamics of their population and environmental
dimensions. This book represents a major step forward in this
recognition, with emphasis on the harmonious balance between
settlements patterns and systems and the natural environment.
The discussion of specific technologies and approaches is
designed to be helpful toward these objectives, and indicative of
the wide range of research, development, and implementation
remaining on the agenda for actions of the international
community in this field.

I have had a profound respect for the importance of well-
conceived human settlements technology research and development ever since my service 20 years ago as director of CINVA, the
Inter-American Housing Center, in Bogotá, Colombia. There,
with the help of a dedicated team, but with only very modest
direct cost, it proved possible to improve substantially several
existing building technologies, especially those having to do
with earth and adobe, the world's most commonly used

★The views expressed are those of the author, and do not represent
official positions.

(environmentally sound) building materials. One example was
the CINVA-RAM machine, a hand-operated stabilized earth block-
maker which was originally designed to fit within the criteria of
a $50 cost limitation and easy portability on muleback or other
transport through roadless territory. This machine, whose direct
development cost and prototype manufacture was less than
$8,000, has now built hundreds of thousands of low-cost
dwellings and schools around the world, and is manufactured
locally, from Ghana to Indonesia. Though it is by no means a
universal answer to production of shelter, the CINVA-RAM has
served as symbol for self-help and mutual-help construction
and community organization efforts in many countries.

Much of the material in this book, well assembled by Gwen
Bell, flows from meetings on community technology and eco-
development, which were initially convoked by the Preparatory
Planning Group (PPG) for the HABITAT Conference, under the
auspices of the UN Environment Program (UNEP). (The
conceptual basis for the meetings was prepared largely by
Alvaro Ortega, and summarized in *HABITAT* 76, a report to the
Executive Director of UNEP by the PPG in December 1973.) The
presentations at these meetings were followed up at the Southeast
Asia Regional Workshop on Environmental and Population
Dimensions of Human Settlements, jointly sponsored in March
1975 by the UN Fund for Population Activities (UNFPA),
UNEP, and the Development Academy of the Philippines. The
Indonesian national Symposium on Human Settlements, held in
Jakarta in July 1975, assisted by the UNDP and by UNEP, helped
to give more emphasis to strategies for human settlements at the
national government level. A fundamental objective throughout
these meetings was to identify and describe selected innovative
solutions for improving the quality of life in human settlements,
especially in such basic fields as shelter, food, transportation,
waste recycling, and wiser use of natural resources.

Finally, UNEP itself convoked in Nairobi in October 1975 an
international advisory group meeting on human settlements
technology, which produced a conceptual framework and guide-

lines for an action program in this field, to be followed up by
meetings at regional levels in the developing countries, and by
the organization and implementation of pilot, demonstration,
and training projects. Such projects will be carried out in special
collaboration with local groups of professionals, producer and
consumer representatives, and key decision-makers.

The basic conclusion of the UNEP advisory-group meeting
was that a concentrated consortium-type effort for the promotion
and extension of an environmentally sound human settlements
technology program at this time would yield great dividends.
The group suggested that the assistance of international
agencies, regional organizations, and foundations for such a
concentrated effort be invited, so that a coordinated and
complementary approach could be developed. This book should
serve as a benchmark and clarion call for the establishment of
a major new program of this type, perhaps comparable to the
highly-successful consortium currently operational in the field
of agricultural research.

It is clear that we have come full circle from the situation
of more than 30 years ago when the United Nations was being
organized. At the UN Conference on International Organization,
held in San Francisco in May 1945, the Greek delegation
pointed out in a special memorandum that "the whole world
will be faced simultaneously with unprecedented housing needs,
demanding the production of technical works to an extent
several times as great as in the postwar period," and proposed a
number of specific areas for technical development with UN
collaboration. In December 1945 the Australian delegation
recommended to the Preparatory Commission of the UN the
establishment of an international center for the exchange of
information on the technical, social, and economic aspects of
housing and town and country planning.

In 1946 the US government suggested the establishment of
an office or unit dealing specifically with international problems
of housing and reconstruction, and in December that year also,
the French delegation proposed the summoning of an inter-

national conference on housing and town planning—*plus ça change...*★

It is not my purpose here to trace the developments concerning international assistance for human settlements over these past 30 years. This history is available in documentation of the UN Center for Housing, Building and Planning, established in 1965 which was the successor to the earlier Housing and Town and Country Planning and the Housing, Building and Planning Branch in the Bureau of Social Affairs of the Department of Economic and Social Affairs of the UN Secretariat in New York. Suffice it to say that this assistance had low priority at both national and intergovernmental levels. It was inadequate in both scope and concept, though much good work was done to establish the foundations for broadened international understanding and action, such as emerged at the UN Conference on the Human Environment, held in Stockholm in June 1972, where the "Planning, Organization and Management of Human Settlements" received major attention.

The recommendations of the Stockholm Conference resulted, of course, in the establishment of the UN Environment Program, whose 58-member Governing Council has consistently demonstrated its deep concern and involvement with the environmental dimensions of human settlements. The Stockholm recommendations, as followed up by the Governing

---

★These suggestions should also be viewed in the context of much earlier international work in this general field. The International Labor Organization had adopted resolutions on the subject dating from 1921/1922, and published a number of basic documents on housing and housing policy through the 1930s. The League of Nations, under its Health Committee, had established a Housing Commission in 1936. By 1946 UNESCO had proposed an international center or clearinghouse on home and community planning. And by December 1946 a special report on a program of international cooperation in housing and urbanism, pointing out the problem and the opportunity and the elements of a first program, was prepared by a consultant, Jacob Crane, and presented to the Honorable Trygve Lie, then Secretary-General of the United Nations.

Council and by the UN General Assembly, have also resulted in three significant actions.

1. Establishment of the UN Habitat and Human Settlements Foundation, which became operational in 1975.
2. Support for HABITAT: the UN Conference on Human Settlements, held in Vancouver in 1976.
3. Development of a Human Settlements Program in UNEP itself.

The three interrelated decisions of UNEP, supported by the complementary efforts of other international agencies and the sympathetic response for action at the national and the extra-national levels now present an unusual opportunity for the development of a global strategy to improve the environmental quality of human settlements on the massive scale required.

Community technology or human settlements technology in its broad sense, forms a keystone of the trilogy required for such a global strategy, linked with both financial and organizational or institutional approaches.

Here we might note the comments of Richard E. Leakey, distinguished anthropologist of the National Museum of Kenya in Nairobi, in HABITAT 76.

Technology should be seen as a critical extension of man's behaviour and this is important from the evolutionary perspective. Two million years ago, we can see evidence for man's technologically patterned activities—returning to a home base, using tools, sharing the work load within a given social unit. The development of man and his place in the eco-systems relates directly to the level of technological skills, and any imbalance will have significant effects on the success of the social unit concerned.

In the present day, we can observe that, for community technology generally, there exists a vast amount of research,

ongoing projects and problem-solving capabilities in all regions
of the world. However, because of lack of communication and
coordination, programs are often duplicated and approaches
fragmented. There has been a resulting incapacity to translate
much existing knowledge into programs at national and regional
levels. This is especially unfortunate now that the world has
become aware of the need for new strategies for energy production, distribution, and utilization at the human settlements
level, and other major considerations within the context of the
new international economic order. Certainly the motto "do more
with less" has also become a major focusing point for all
community technology development, especially with regard to
use of nonrenewable natural resources within the "inner" and
"outer" limits of consideration of humanity's minimum needs,
including shelter requirements, and the support constraints of
the biosphere.

The UNEP Advisory Group on Human Settlements Technology took note of the challenge that over the next 30 years the
governments of developing countries in particular will face the
task of providing jobs, food, housing, physical facilities, and
social services for another 2,800 million inhabitants (or more
than the population of the entire world in 1950), in both urban
and rural areas.* Any effort to deal with this situation must
obviously involve multidisciplinary approaches if environmentally sound communities are to result. Moreover, the
objectives must be specific and well-categorized.

Certain problems of settlements are common worldwide;
others are unique. Some general global categories can be
defined, but specific priorities must be made regionally or even
subregionally; while at the global level, workable program areas
should be identified in preparation for action.

Existing knowledge and research should be fully utilized
while also stressing new and promising innovative approaches.
The dynamic character of change often quickly renders obsolete

---

*Report of the UNEP Advisory Group Meeting on Human Settlements
Technology, Kenyatta Conference Center, Nairobi, 6 to 8 October 1975.

existing knowledge, but it should be better disseminated, and applied while it is still relevant.

The UNEP Group agreed that the main objectives of a determined new effort for development and improvement of human settlements technology should be to

(a) Identify a global network of leading institutions in the field of human settlements technology, which will be organized on an ecosystem and regional basis.

(b) Establish the necessary mechanisms for coordinating and promoting the activities of these institutions, (research, information, implementation of projects).

(c) Collect, disseminate and make all data in the field readily available.

(d) Promote the use of environmentally sound technologies which, due to their very nature, will help countries and communities become self-reliant.

The above objectives should be seen also as tools to make it increasingly possible for nations to plan their destiny, as visualized under the emerging concept of a new international economic order. A human settlements approach is a key conceptual instrument for this process, and indeed it has been said that national planning through strategies for settlements is a means of humanizing and socializing the whole development process.

The human settlements approach sees man—in totality—in work, in play, at home, and in relationship with nature and the environment. Its objective is to ensure the spread of development efforts—the quality of life—to the people. The major components are to promote productivity, through spatial considerations, and public service delivery systems, for human welfare. A key issue in many countries is that of space, and therefore land—with the population dynamics and environmental dimensions—becomes the integrating factor in planning. For while population and urbanization rates increase, land does not, nor does the biosphere of this *only one earth*. Rational management of this resource—and providing land for people and their activities—is both the problem, and the means by which solutions can be found.

The approaches to planning for human settlements have both national and international implications. On the national side, more positive planning and action for human settlements can accelerate the development process with greater social equity and also serve as a means of stimulating participation of the people and greater civic and environmental responsibility. It can mobilize new resources—the people's energies—as well as fostering savings and opening channels of investment within broader human settlement concepts.

On the international scene, the community and human settlements approach within national framework plans offers a means of focusing and integrating technical and financial assistance.

On all fronts, we have the profound obligation to manage wisely our existing environmental resources—land, space, water, air, energy—and to constantly innovate and to recycle so as to do more with less, if our communities are to be truly livable. This will require immense efforts to foster innovating technology and to implant new systems and techniques for human settlements development, including industrial and food production and other systems to maintain the balance of man in harmony with his environment.

My conviction is that each country has a great deal to contribute. Each has tremendous problems but there are also tremendous resources of people, land, space, water, air and energy. The right synergetic combinations will produce significant achievements for human welfare; but for this to happen, the use of the appropriate community technologies will be all-important. The private sector must contribute extensively to this process. There must be more general agreement on objectives and the rules of the game so that all can participate and contribute more productively and efficiently for the improvement of human settlements within national framework plans and concepts.

In conclusion, with a 30-year not-too-successful *history* of international involvement and assistance for human settlements improvement, and a 30-year *perspective and challenge* of providing environmentally sound human settlements for a doubled population of earthlings, it is clear that we are in a swift midstream of potential triumph or disaster. We now know the directions, but it will take all our determination and skills at national, regional, and local levels to achieve the planning and mobilization of resources and practical utilization and implementation of the broad spectrum of community technologies now available for human settlements development on an ecosystem basis.

This may involve the need for substantial reorganization of many of our traditional institutions for communication, training and education, if they are to remain relevant and adapt to the new concepts and realities. This book points the way to the future in this field; the time has now come for careful organization, programing and implementation.

Introduction

GWEN BELL

There is no single policy that deals more adequately
with full resource use, an abatement of pollution, and
even the search for more labor-intensive activities
than a planned and purposive strategy for human
settlements.

> —Barbara Ward and René Dubos,
> *Only One Earth*, p. 180

Although some politicians, some industrialists, some
naturalists and others would like to create a
dichotomy between human settlements and the natural environment, there is none. Each contribution to this book provides
supportive evidence and outlines proposals for organizing
human settlements in concert with nature.

The global environment—as many have pointed out—has
been modified to the extent that the natural equilibrium is
unknown. But the cumulative knowledge of mankind has been
increasing with regard to our planetary systems—the earth's
atmosphere, its surface, its interior, and its flora and fauna. In
cases in which this knowledge has been applied to settlements,
the population has benefited. Until Tokyo's building regulations
were modified for earthquake conditions, its population lived in
considerable fear. Understanding the local atmospheric
conditions that manufacture smog in the Los Angeles basin led
the citizens to take action with regard to automotive pollution.

In Reykjavik, the gloomy and cold capital of Iceland, the zoning ordinance positions houses on the southern exposure to maximize the limited sunlight and make living conditions more pleasant. These cases and others described in this book illustrate synergies between settlements and nature, creating environments that can have negative or positive effects on mankind. Because settlements are not only local but also universal phenomena around the globe, the audience for the strategies outlined herein ranges from people with purely local to those with international concern.

There are examples and principles relevant to people in all environments. For the peoples living in industrialized nations, who must become more and more energy conscious and environmentally concerned, ways are shown to renew old settlements and to build new ones in concert with nature. For the peoples of the developing countries, where the necessity to build settlements is the greatest, and capital is the shortest, frameworks are outlined that will allow incremental development of settlement systems, using labor-intensive methods and inter-mediate technologies. And finally, for the peoples blessed with an abundance of energy, models are pointed out for building new settlements with advanced technologies that provide for human needs without destructiveness to the environment.

The ideas are specific, even when dealing with outlines for planning, and none are overly complex, even when dealing with advanced technologies. The material is presented so that any council member, legislator, concerned citizen, or student can understand it.

Some readers will discover different proposals that are appropriate to the problems of their own area. Other readers will learn about exciting new developments that will stretch their minds. And still other readers who are concerned with global strategies will use the articles as supporting evidence.

Each author was selected because he is at the forefront in his field and is able to present explicit proposals. The individual strategies are grouped into three parts; the first establishes the framework for considering settlement systems and natural systems. The last two parts interchange the dependent variables: first, the organization of nature in terms of settlements, and then the organization of settlements in terms of nature.

Buckminster Fuller leads off Part I with his continually fresh approach to holistically building the future. But he admits that whether the world will ever achieve the promise of a brighter future depends on the decision taken now for the next 25 years. Specific policies that can be, and in a few places have been, implemented are spelled out in the remainder of the first part.

The articles in the last part are specific. All the proposals in Part II emphasize the importance of the production of food, materials, and energy close to the area of consumption in settlements. For examples, Taylor Pryor describes a closed system of aquaculture for the tropics; C. A. Morrison illustrates the principles of solar heating; other authors treat topics equally to the point. These are concrete ways in which many regions can move from the "cowboy" economy of the past in which the wealth of a city was based on its exports, to the "spaceship" economy of the future in which wealth is dependent on how wisely inhabitants provide for themselves.

The closing part of the book emphasizes high technology solutions that have low environmental impacts. These are investments which have few external diseconomies and low long-run costs. They are not designed for the industrial city of the past, but for the environmental city of the future.

PART I

Achieving More Than Peaceful Coexistence: Synthesis of Settlement Systems and Natural Systems

Introduction

GWEN BELL

From the outset of the establishment of the United
Nations Environment Program (UNEP) there has
been a false dichotomy between human settlements and nature.
This division, however, is being reinforced by its very
acceptance at the policymaking level. The Fifth Report of the
United States Council on Environmental Quality stated:

> The differences in philosophy between the developing and
> developed nations . . . (were evident) at the first session of the
> Governing Council. In the perception of developing coun-
> tries, the major environmental problems relate to the lack of
> economic development, and they want UNEP to concentrate
> on activities that relate to and support such development.
> The developed countries, in contrast, are more concerned
> about the impact of man on natural systems and want
> UNEP to play a major role in improving our knowledge of
> the global environment and coordinating efforts to manage
> and protect it. The Action Plan reflects the interests of both
> groups.

But these concerns are not conflicting. The unifying factor
for "nature" and "settlements" is space in the global system. A
Pete Seeger folksong of the sixties tied it together. It started,

> The faucets are dripping in old New York City,
> The faucets are dripping and nobody's caring...

and went on to describe the interrelationships of the landlord in
a Miami Beach hotel, the reservoir in New York State, the poor
tenant trying to pay the water bill, the inept public works
engineers, the misery of slum living, the rain cycle and the
reservoir, and so on. Similarly, as a young child, I can remember
being fascinated with a bonfire and asking my parents, "Where
does it go?"

"Away, into the air."

The next day, not entirely satisfied, I asked, "Where is
away?" From folk wisdom and a child's perception, it is clear
that all must be one.

Then, as the awareness of the complexity of life grows, the
multidimensionality of each element takes on more and more
importance. Each subspecialization of understanding of the
human system, the heart or the lungs; each specialization of the
settlement system, transportation or cultural centers; each
subspecialization of the natural system, feral dogs, algae, or
shale, can provide a lifetime career.

But, simultaneously, the adult who refines his specialization
is also a citizen of a community and the world. As such, he is
expected to deal with issues, outside his expertise, where his
knowledge comes from the front page of the newspaper, the
five-minute newscast, or a politician's speech. All these presentations simplify the issues; much of the multidimensionality is
lost; and only the sharp distinctions are left. The poor are
separated from the rich, nature from man, artists from scientists,
the employed from the unemployed. The constant use of these
categorizations leads to divisiveness on our small planet.

The five authors in this part bring out the inherent oneness
of the environment and outline new approaches and new
specializations in accordance with the underlying philosophy
that treats the earth as a precious habitat for all living things.

Preparing for a Small Town World

R. BUCKMINSTER FULLER

In my lifetime of 78 years I have seen a great deal of change. I grew up in an era when man traveled primarily on foot, horse, and bicycle, and was very local.

The East (with 51 percent of humanity) and Europe and Africa (with 29 percent of humanity) are very remote from the Americas (with 12 percent North and 7 percent South, respectively), or were, before the advent of the aeroplane. (See Fig. 1) Seventy years ago, it took three months to get to India. My latest trip to India last year was quicker than my first trip from Boston to New York as a child. I can reach India by telephone in a couple of minutes, so I find the world completely integrated. In 1961, three jet planes outperformed the Queen Mary in one-third the time for one-half the price, so the ocean became obsolete as a means of getting from here to there. The era of surface travel completely stopped without people realizing what had happened. We have tumbled into one small-town world.

The standard Mercator projection was developed for the world oriented to ocean communication. All the nations were very remote then, and could be connected only by ship. The oceans and the trade winds framed a merry-go-round, which

Fig. 1. Four Worlds

World One we know little about. Each invisible dot X represents X persons, or one percent of humanity before 5,000,000 B.C. By the fastest travel in World One, the remotest from one another could not reach one another, and did not know of one another's existence.

World Two was an east-west axis water-travel-divided world. Each small dot represents 16 million people, or one percent of humanity in 1900. By the fastest possible travel in 1900, the remotest from one another small dots were 90 days apart.

World Three is a north-south axis air-travel-divided world.
Each large dot represents 40 million people, or one percent of
humanity in 1975. By the fastest possible travel in 1975, the
remotest from one another large dots are 2 days apart.

World Four is an omnidirectional electromagnetic-travel-
divided world. Each invisible dot represents Y million people,
or one percent of humanity in 2000 A.D. By the fastest possible
travel in 2000 A.D., the remotest from one another (invisible)
dots are one-seventh of one second of time apart.

R. Buckminster Fuller © 1975

the ships took advantage of. The masters of the seas were those who controlled the southern tips of Africa, Australia, New Zealand, and South America, which all ships had to pass to get from ocean to ocean and to rejoin the merry-go-round shipping routes. But the masters of ships controlled the wealth of our earth. The Mercator projection was appropriate enough for earth when people sailed around its middle, which it distorts the least, but it is very inappropriate for our air-borne times. It ignores the poles and distorts the polar regions, showing Greenland three times bigger than Australia.

My Dymaxion map (Fig. 2) presents a truer picture of the earth, showing Australia as the continent it is, four times as

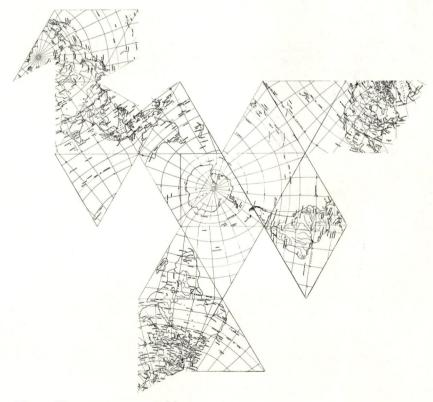

Fig. 2. The water-ocean world

big as Greenland. You can see the whole world at once, with no visible distortion of the relative shape or size of any of the parts. If you show 100 percent of any data against this background, it will read properly.

If you rearrange the pieces of the Dymaxion map (Fig. 3) with the North Pole at the center, you will see a one-world island. That is the map of our present era. Eighty-five percent of all the land in the world is north of the equator. Less than 10 percent of humanity lives south of the equator. Ninety percent of the world's people can reach each other via the circle air routes over the Pole without going near the Atlantic, Pacific, or Indian oceans. The old east/west, north/south separations, with each nation looking out for itself, are no longer valid. The fragmentation of the world into nations that was logical yesterday, when men were inherently divided by time and space, is changing.

We have utter intimacy of communication, and willy-nilly, we have complete integration of the interests of humanity.

I no longer think of underdeveloped and small nations that need help, and big rich ones that must help them. I see all mankind being integrated into one world pattern. The mobile young are beginning to live all around the world. As a visiting professor at universities around the world, I find that the tendency of students is to regard themselves as world citizens, which is what they want to be. Students from New Guinea and from Africa who go to Europe and America for training, want, naturally, to go back to their villages to help their people, but they are beginning to find that the village and the family at home want to become part of the greater world too. No doubt there will be a very long period of transition, but there has to be accommodation to this new way humanity is beginning to think and to live.

Economic Revolutions

I was born in a society in which 90 percent of the people had to live on farms to grow their own food. We learned ways of getting food into cans, and of using refrigerated transport to

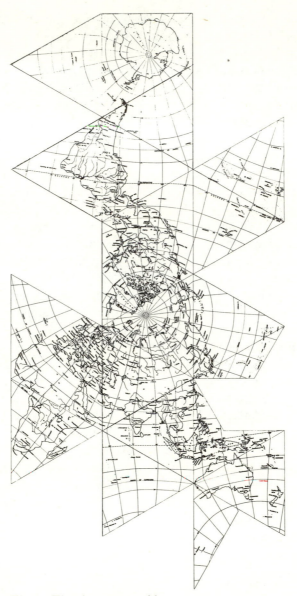

Fig. 3. The air-ocean world

reach people anywhere. We learned to handle great farms mechanically, almost without human intervention. But we have not changed our accounting system, based on a seasonal agrarian economy, even though the year has nothing at all to do with the industrial cycle. The tasks to be done in our industrial economies may run into 30-, 40-, or 50-year cycles. People don't comprehend something that is going to take forty or fifty years to develop. It doesn't help much to repair yesterday or try to make the kind of buildings we used to have—things that are very logical if you are going to stay put on your land, and have a very permanent kind of building there.

Most of the 90 percent of humanity which used to be on the farm has come into the cities, hoping for employment and the good life. The city wasn't designed to take care of all these people. Populations are continuing to shift from country to city and city to megacity.

Men came to cities in the past because there were harbors and warehouses, and that was the place to find jobs; but the jobs have deployed out from the cities, as far as physical production and retail commerce goes. Big cities, instead of being warehouses and centers for the exchange of physical goods, are developing into metaphysical exchanges. You find New York City, for example, being taken over by the great universities, the United Nations, and the like, for the interchange of ideas, or by value exchanges like the banks and the stock markets, that deal in paper abstractions, bonds, stocks, money, credit. The big cities are processing the metaphysical, and the physical is increasingly processed outside the cities.

Yesterday Is Obsolete

One must understand that much of yesterday is really obsolete. I can think of ingenious ameliorating things to do, but what we really need is fundamental change. For instance, our working assumption is that we were all born naked and helpless, with an instinctive need to take on fuel. Time and again, thinkers have discovered that there is not enough fuel in the world to support life. All the great ideologies still operate on the assumption that

there is an inherent inadequacy of life support. That is why
there are political parties, which each say "we cannot guarantee
that you will really like our system, but we have the fairest,
most logical way of dealing with fundamental inadequacy."
Nations fight to gain control over the supplies of fuel. The
appropriations for arms of the USA, USSR, NATO, and China,
year after year amount to $200 billion. Not only man's wealth,
but his highest capabilities, are focused on how to destroy
rather than how to make or enhance life.

We have been assuming humanity must fail because there
is not enough food to go around. We seem to assume that
everybody is supposed to be a failure. The term "earning a
living" implies that you have to prove you are an exception in
order to be allowed to live.

Yet I can tell you that it is completely feasible to take care
of all humanity, at the highest standard of living that anyone
has ever known, without anybody's sacrificing or taking
advantage of anyone else. It can be done by 1985 with resources
we have already mined and knowledge we already have. It is
now visible, if we are willing to accept a completely new basic
assumption, that man is designed to be a success like the rest of
the universe, and not a failure.

What do you need for human beings? We are all born on
a spaceship beautifully equipped with a biosphere, water, air,
and so on. But Spaceship Earth is running out of equipment
and supplies. There is no air to breathe, no water to drink, and
no wires or connections. How to keep life going?

Governments may engage in space programs for the wrong
reasons, for military purposes, but the inadvertent result has
been to teach us what human beings really need to keep on
living.

The equipment required to recirculate water and to keep
life going for six men for a year in a space capsule will fit in one
large airplane suitcase, weighing 70 pounds. This is enough
equipment to do away with all the sewers and the water-supply
systems to keep six men alive anywhere in the universe; which
means that you can keep them on board the planet earth, where
things are very much more favorable, at less expense.

Pollution = Misplaced Resources

I find the words "pollution" and so forth words of great ignorance. We have in our physical universe 92 chemical elements, and every one of them is essential to the eternal regeneration of the eternally intertransforming regenerative universe. One of the most expensive steps in the mining process is to separate the part you want from the matrix. People take out this part and get rid of the rest, calling it waste. The power company sells electricity and has a great deal of by-product it really doesn't want, called sulphur. The amount of sulphur coming annually out of smokestacks all around the world, and polluting their environs, is exactly the amount of sulphur we expensively take out of the earth in order to make automobiles. Now just before it emerges from the smokestack the sulphur is highly concentrated. After it comes out of the stack, it fuses with all the other gases; it costs a fantastic amount ever to separate it out again. In fact, everything that comes out of a nozzle or a smokestack has a very high concentration of some valuable chemical or other. In our society private companies are reluctant to do anything about this. They say they cannot compete in industry if they must go through this expensive retrieval process. Society therefore must assert its right to the air, and to the resources misplaced in it, and insist that the companies are responsible for returning these resources to society. Every company around the world should be required to recover these resources, perhaps compensated by tax rebates, and return them to the governments. The governments will then be able to stockpile sulphur and the other valuable products, all of which are very much needed.

We must stop talking about pollution and start talking about very valuable resources. In the end, it will pay to do the right thing from the beginning, particularly when the chemicals are already sorted out and ready to be reused.

The Greatest Revolution

We are going to have the greatest revolution in humanity: either it is going to be a bloody revolution in which everybody

loses or a designed revolution in which everybody comes out
with confidence. The possibilities are terribly exciting when
people do have confidence and think about how to do more
with less, and then do things much better than previously
imagined.

It is not a matter of who's going to make the most money,
but how to make humanity a success. That is the big challenge.
There must be no compromise at all in bringing out the best we
have in us. Somebody has to attend to the exploration of what
are the tactical factors and what are the critical design inputs.
We now know enough about how to make our world work so
that we can choose to cross this threshold successfully.

If we are going to be able to take care of humanity, not
just get ready for war, then we must find out how to control our
environment. What equipment do we need to do it? Humanity
must achieve the success it was designed to be. But we are at
the point where there could be a stillbirth. Nothing is so critical
as birth, and whether the world survives it or not depends on
our integrity. We have enough technological know-how at our
disposal to give everyone a decent life, and release humanity to
do what it is supposed to be doing—that is, really using our
minds, doing really extraordinary things, not just coping with
survival. You and I are given a hunger drive so that we will be
sure to take on fuel and regenerate our bodies; we are given a
drive to procreate so that mankind will be regenerated; we are
also given minds. I find the conditioned reflexes of humanity
are not being challenged at all; we keep playing games of how
to get on in the world. But the function of mankind is to think,
and we are *going to have to exercise this responsibility*.

Rethinking a Framework for Settlement Planning

ERNEST WEISSMAN

The impact of scientific and technological progress of population trends and ways of producing a living continues to rapidly change human societies from their predominantly rural, agricultural base to an urban, industrial base.

Through industrialization, city regions are being formed as new kinds of entities that are cities in the socioeconomic sense and regions in the geographic and administrative sense. The concept of the mutually productive interaction of economic growth, human development, and the quality of the environment, which is so essential to these new entities, though accepted in theory, is far from being generally recognized and even further from being practiced.

For the first time in history, as a world society, we possess the science, the technology, and the required resources, with which to substantially influence the direction of further development, the quality of the environment, and the nature of society itself. If the GNP as a measure of development is replaced by NEW (National Economic Welfare), the public could trade, for instance, half a percent of conventional GNP yearly growth in order to achieve perhaps an extra quarter percent rate of NEW growth and buy a good bargain.

There is consequently an urgent need for meaningful participation by the citizens and political leaders with the planners and administrators in the complex process of conceiving, projecting, implementing, and continuously expanding development intended for the benefit of the given area's people. This in turn may humanize development by itself.

The most often stated objective of development is social progress, but social progress is not, as we know from experience, an automatic consequence of development. To achieve social progress, a nation has to devote a share of its wealth to social development, and plan for equitable distribution of the benefits that it can offer. Social progress and economic growth, the environment and the development of human settlements are closely connected processes in the development of our societies. Their interaction determines the direction and pace of development, but how different societies use these processes in their development, how they distribute the benefits obtained through deliberate development, and what attitudes they assume towards the environment is determined by the value systems and the political process of decision-making that their respective cultures have developed. In any of these systems, a unified socioeconomic environmental and administrative management approach to planning and planning implementation should be adopted.

Five Preconceived Ideas to Overcome

Historic determinism holds that all development must follow the patterns evolved in the industrialized societies despite the fact that these have generated many social and environmental phenomena that are detrimental to the human qualities of life.

Economic determinism holds that, in the context of development, economics is an exact science, like the natural sciences that seek to understand and perhaps harness nature's immutable laws, but cannot change them. Economic determinists say that economic efficiency motivates and guides development, which in turn must produce economic benefits as large and fast as is feasible, regardless of social cost, human hardship, or environmental damage, so that the material benefits of development reach more people in the long run.

Technological determinism holds that effective use of modern technology requires ever greater concentrations of production and services and even larger agglomerations of people and facilities, in order to benefit from scale economies. In this argument external economies that pollute the environment and create new costs are seldom counted.

The center peripheral theory holds that for the sake of economic efficiency there must be a concentration of production and people, of economic power and business, of national wealth and political power in the dominant cities and regions in individual countries and in the dominant nations of the world. This concentration occurs at the expense of the marginal people, the peripheral areas, of individual countries and the poor nations in general, as a phase in the long-term process of national and world-wide economic development.

The theory of equilibrium holds that the free market is a self-regulating socioeconomic system in which the interplay of supply and demand automatically corrects any imblanaces among the different factors influencing development, such as investment, production and distribution. There is no need, therefore, for societies to regulate these processes for the purpose of diminishing the differences between the rich and the poor or reducing the growing gap between the affluent nations and those locked in underdevelopment.

Adjusting to New Concepts

The settlement system can be the vehicle for adjusting the economic and social aspects of development to each other. The mainstream of progress in the economic, social, political, and physical spheres have taken place in settlement systems. In future the function of distributing these benefits more equitably will also take place in settlement systems.

In the past, growth has conflicted with the natural environmental systems, in terms of the capacity of the ecosystem to absorb or recycle the wastes produced by man-made development. But if settlement systems are looked at as a multitude of open systems, they can be related to the total system of our one earth.

Having accepted the principle or the idea of the planet earth as one unit from the environmental point of view, we should now start on the more difficult road of accepting planet earth as one in the economic sense, and in the sense of keeping peace and not blowing ourselves up.

National Planning for Human Settlements

JOSÉ CONRADO BENITEZ

Economic growth spelled out in gross national product does not measure the welfare of people living in communities. Considerations, which in traditional economics are related to those of the business firm, can and must be translated to relate to the community.

Because this new approach is very difficult to introduce into traditional governmental structures, the Government of the Philippines set up a special Presidential Task Force to implement it. An executive decree organized some 17 different agencies, involved in a whole range of sectoral concerns such as public works, housing, and pollution control, with a working secretariat from the Development Academy of the Philippines.

The mandate of the Task Force was to effect a national program which would serve as a framework for all human settlements, from metropolitan Manila to small-scale selected projects, and at the same time, effect a national program on housing. Since it was instructed to accomplish its task as fast as possible, there was simultaneous concern for the new broad concept of national development based on human settlements and for effecting practical action strategies that would satisfy decision-makers and solve some urgent problems.

The task force demonstrates a method of relating technical problems to institutional arrangements and policymaking problems. First, there is a mandate from the highest governmental level, a presidential directive. Second, all the different agencies concerned are involved in the task force. But, as you and I know, when some 17 different agencies are put together you don't get very much done. That is why we set up a completely separate secretariat within the Development Academy of the Philippines (DAP). A young staff was brought to a live-in situation and consultants were recruited from all the different agencies. The full-time working secretariat reported to the Task Force, which recruited personnel from all governmental agencies and contracted with individuals who would be able to participate in project teams that would get the action and the programs of the Task Force going. In three months, the Task Force came out with its first report, which involved identification of the emerging concepts and issues of human settlements, a preliminary national framework, a framework for Metro Manila, and the identification of housing problems and programs. Since then, the Task Force has been expanded into a Zoning and Planning Commission and has become involved in more programmatic concerns.

The critical issue is area development and community technology, not a transfer of various specific packages of innovation. What is needed is the mobilization of resources within a given area in order to produce innovational packages. Direct involvement comes in area management, or area mobilization of resources. For example, the government had allocated money for medium- and small-scale industry and human settlements. The academy mobilized 80 students and two professionals to locate prospective entrepreneurs and farmers to work through the project development feasibility stage, and link them to banking institutions to tap the available money supplies. It is this intermediary role in creating new institutional arrangements that we find most lacking.

Unless we can effect new institutional arrangements, many of the things that we talk about will not really come about. The most important thing is to determine the action strategies that can be used as leverage to effect a full-scale program that would reorient some traditional attitudes (be they in technology or pollution) to bring about rural transformation, and the consideration of human communities as the object and concern of development.

The Vision of a New Society in the Philippines*

The Philippines, though not in a "crisis" situation with regard to environmental deterioration or food shortage, has nevertheless been experiencing structural changes that threaten to worsen the existing low quality of life of the majority of Filipinos. This has to do primarily with the fast rate of population increase. Significantly, this increase is occurring in a few, but relatively densely populated areas, particularly around Manila. It has resulted in urban blight, a housing shortage, pollution of inland waters, inadequacy of public utilities, poverty, and a general lowering of the quality of life.

The country also had its share of calamities. The 1972 floods caused unprecedented damage. Rice supply fell to a critical level in 1973, and white corn had to be substituted in the people's diet. The oil crisis likewise had telling effects on consumer prices. The country has faced up to these crises; nonetheless, this is probably the most opportune time to plan more rationally for the future of the country. While conditions have not reached critical levels, there is need to manage our numbers effectively, our resources wisely, our food supply efficiently, and our life-support systems intelligently.

A Framework Plan

A solution to some of the problems of development can be achieved through a locational or spatial approach. The organized and systematic distribution in space of activities contributing to development means a more efficient arrangement, which in turn

*This section is extracted from *Human Settlements: The Vision of a New Society*, vol. 2, *A Framework Plan for the Nation*, Task Force on Human Settlements. (Quezon City: Development Academy of the Philippines, 1974.)

maximizes benefits and minimizes the negative effects of
unplanned growth.

A framework plan is intended to effect the proper spatial
relationships of people and their activities; it is meant to utilize
space and physical resources in the most efficient and optimal
manner. Framework plans can be formulated for various levels.
National plans present broad strategies for development, but do
not attempt detailed plans for the location of shops, houses, and
factories.

A national framework plan provides a guide for development planning. It lends support to economic and social development plans that need to utilize space. In doing so, it serves to
integrate the development process on a common platform: land.
It likewise provides an institutional framework by providing
a reference point that links the planning process and its
implementation.

A framework plan assumes another role: it provides policymakers with bases for decisions and for ordering priorities.

Certain policy goals have guided the formulation of the
framework plan. The primary objective of human settlements
planning is to ensure to the majority of people the benefits of
development. Planned settlements can better provide facilities
and services, and better promote a living environment that will
enhance the well-being of the community. As a consequence of
unplanned growth, the Philippine experience of "development"
has actually evolved into an overconcentration of people,
activities, technology, and governmental services in the Manila
area. Almost three-fourths of the total number of Philippine
manufacturing establishments are located in the Manila Bay
Region; they generated some 65 percent of total family income
in 1971. The same pattern of uneven distribution of consumer
items prevails. Outside Manila a handful of secondary urban
centers enjoys far fewer benefits than Manlia; the rest of the
country does not seem to share in development.

This is a classic pattern. Though gross national product may
increase, the benefits are shared by only a few, usually by
families residing in the primate city. Unless a better distribution

of the fruits of development is ensured, the country will remain basically underdeveloped.

With the foregoing thoughts in mind, the following goals serve as objectives in formulating the framework plan for the country.

Goal 1: Resources

In view of the relatively untapped natural resources of the country, the objective of resource utilization is proposed. The initial thrust should be toward self-sufficiency in food and related industries. This will entail identifying prime agricultural land and areas most suited for fishing and livestock production, in relation to regional projections of food demands.

Mining and forestry resources, which are in relative abundance, should be exploited, after due ecological considerations, for the economic development of the country.

Other resources that need further studies include water and energy sources. Geothermal and hydroelectric sources of energy should be identified and settlements planned in relation to them.

Goal 2: the Countryside

This approach emphasizes not only the initiation of development programs throughout the country, but more important, the retention of the benefits of programs and resources in the various parts of the country. It is *not* rural development if most of the profits of mining operations in Cebu, or of wood processing in Cotabato, go to Manila. Utilization of the resources of the countryside should mean employment for local people, better services and facilities, more consumer items, in short, a higher standard of living. It is only in this way that the majority of Filipinos will be able to enjoy the fruits of of development.

Goal 3: Regional Integration

Resource utilization and rural development should be tied in with the objective of regional integration. The geographic diversity of the country suggests that a regional approach is

most feasible, economical, and efficient. It is needed to lesson
the importance and dependence of other regions on Manila. In
the past, situations arose wherein local governments interacted
more frequently with Manila than with neighboring provinces.
Integration will necessitate improving linkages within regions as
well as with areas other than Manila.

A decentralization of functions and activities will also mean
initiating local leadership and responsibility. The goal is toward
building integrated and self-contained communities, with their
own unique and distinct personalities as regions.

The studies that serve as the bases of this framework plan
include an extensive survey of existing conditions, especially of
development potentials of the country. Land capability was
analyzed to serve as a basis for determining land use. Projected
demand requirements for food and its land requirements were
used in determining projected land uses. An urban settlement
study served as the basis for a growth center strategy. Development strategies are presented for the country in terms of
development potentials of regions.

Urban Settlements

Settlements are used in this study to serve as a starting
point for the framework plan. This stems from various considerations. Foremost is the fact that settlements are, logically,
the unit of analysis and the focus of human gatherings. Second,
the goals enunciated call for a policy of dispersed development.
Foci of development throughout the country, therefore, need to
be identified.

The basic problems revolve around the primacy of Manila,
to which emigration from the countryside is directed primarily.
This trend is unlikely to diminish unless deliberate efforts are
made to make other areas attractive. People migrate to urban
centers seeking better opportunities, and services and facilities
generally characterized as urban. If migration centers on a
search for urban qualities, it would be impractical to propose
nonurban alternatives. This, however, does not mean total
disregard of rural areas. Growth centers are being identified to

serve as focal points for the development of the rural hinter-
lands.

The effective implementation of a policy of dispersed
development necessitates establishing other centers capable of
attracting and absorbing population. Migration usually occurs
in response to economic changes. To disperse population, a key
element revolves on the employment-generating capacity of
centers outside Manila. Based on experiences of other countries,
economies of scale for industries, commerce and services are
achieved in centers with populations ranging from 250,000 to
750,000. It may therefore be economically more efficient for the
government to assign first priority to developing such centers.
Assuming a period of 25 years, development can be channeled to
the larger centers for the first 5 to 10 years. Other areas can then
be improved and the growth nodes subjected to similar concentrated developmental stimuli. Over the 25-year period, a
sizable number of growth centers should come into existence in
different parts of the country. The likely effect of the establishment or expansion of growth centers in redistributing population and economic activity should occur. (Fig. 4)

In pinpointing growth centers, emphasis was placed on
existing urban settlements in order to maximize whatever
investments exist in these centers. Thus, settlement size was
utilized as a primary criterion. Differences in sizes of settlements
reveal differences in the nature of the hierarchical organization
and these in turn, relate to developmental variations. Size, likewise, provides a clue to the intangible attractions in terms of
potentials, of different settlements. The steps taken to determine
the major urban settlements are listed below.

1. Using settlements with a minimum of 5,000 urban popu-
    lation as the sample from which the final selection would
    be made.

2. Scoring these settlements on the following factors:
    regional capital: 40 points
    settlements with at
        least 50,000 population: 10 points

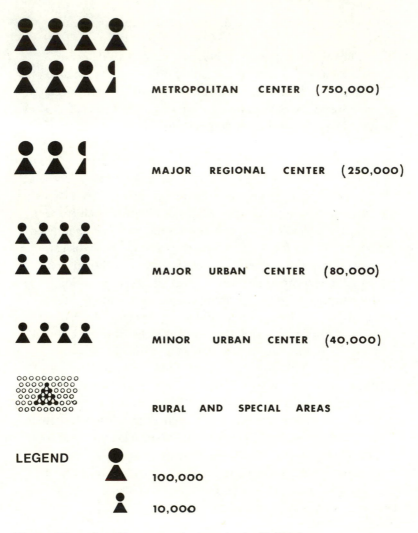

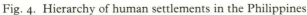

Fig. 4. Hierarchy of human settlements in the Philippines

provincial capitals: 10 points
chartered cities: 10 points
municipalities with at least 5,000 urban population:
    5 points

3. Ranking the settlements by the above scores in relation to other settlements on regional and national scales.

4. Analyzing the scores of settlements, functional interdependencies, and population projections to the year 2000. Settlements were compared with others on regional and national scales.

Applying this scheme of population, five levels of settlements were determined.

Level 1: Metropolitan center of national and international importance. This type of settlement is projected to reach a million population by the year 2000, and may comprise a major city and its outlying districts of satellite communities.

Level 2: Regional and subregional centers are projected to reach at least a population of 251,000 to 750,000 by the year 2000. Regional centers are designated administrative headquarters for regions. They are usually the seat of regional offices of government agencies. The subregional centers are not administrative units, but offer a complete range of urban services and facilities.

Level 3: Major urban centers are potential growth centers. They are projected to reach populations of 81,000 to 250,000. A range of urban activities are likewise available in such centers. Resource frontiers and other leading developmental areas fall under this category.

Level 4: Minor urban centers are less developed. They may be designated agricultural services centers. They have potentials for development as intermediate-sized centers capable of absorbing migration flows to the large urban centers.

The Value of Community Self-Help

FREDERICK GUTHEIM

In preindustrial societies indigenous organic communities existed as the natural condition. These have been sacrificed and negated during the industrialization in the nineteenth century. These organic communities were the product of centuries of trial and error, cultural refinement, and human adjustment. They illustrate a capability that should be maintained and strengthened rather than sacrificed, compromised, and even lost.

The concept that governments exist to do things for people was once a great idea, but now it needs to be challenged. For the idea that a city should be organized primarily to make it convenient and efficient to do things for people, we must substitute the idea that it should facilitate people's doing things for themselves.

What is it, in the transposition from the organic community to the urban setting, that has obliged us to sacrifice this capability? How can people be organized, and communities strengthened in the ability to do things for themselves?

Motivation is of primary importance. Self-help in building has been successful in rural programs. We've got to find some way to establish the same motivation in community improvement in urban programs.

The importance of the small community also deserves acknowledgement. Much of the initial apprehension of social unrest in squatter settlements has disappeared, and their capacity for self-government can be credited. A greater degree of self-sufficiency in both resource conservation and recycling and in the social and economic realm is possible.

The assumption of the benefits of growth can be looked at in terms of their potential in developing countries. The capacity to measure social costs and social indicators is increasing. Once we start looking at city growth in terms of a number of autonomous communities, instead of the unifying metropolitan system, it should be possible to see growth in incremental terms, building one community after another, each relatively complete as it goes along, with a different city structure emerging in consequence.

Finally, there is the question of participation. Until there can actually be created some kind of local power base in the autonomous community, no one will have faith in the ability of that community to face existing policymakers with the confidence it should have.

This is a very crude model of an alternative to the modern western city. But it is incorrect to conclude that the progression of specialization, growth complexity and larger measures of governmental coordination and control that have led to the Western urban condition today are the only route to development. The developing countries should pioneer rather than simply follow the earlier route. As developed countries turn to alternatives for the failing city, they are much more likely to learn from experiences of this kind than from projecting their own errors upon the rest of the world.

PART II

Producing Food, Water, and Energy for Settlements

Introduction

GWEN BELL

The sun provides the daily income within which humanity has to budget itself. When we mine from the earth's interior we are taking savings from the bank. Since these funds have been readily accessible, we have come to depend upon them and consider them almost inexhaustible.

But mankind has had a few scares, and it is becoming evident that the bank accounts are running low. As a result, alternatives are being explored for ways to live within, rather than beyond, our daily solar income. Instead of mining for agricultural fertilizer, instead of draining underground water beds, and instead of tapping the oils and gases deep within the earth, the proposals in this part illustrate ways of better using solar energy to produce food, water, and energy for human use.

You might say to yourself, "There is nothing new in this. It just means returning to the simpler life of our grandfathers." But it doesn't. The numbers of people that need to be provided for and the level of their expectations demand much more. Furthermore, these demands can be met by innovative ways that use solar energy much more intensively. These methods are dependent on sophisticated societies with advanced information systems.

Food

The present food chain, from the field to the dinner table, is highly inefficient. Big cities in industrialized countries have preempted surrounding agricultural land for urban development, pushing the food producers farther and farther away from the urban market. Numerous middlemen have been introduced, each one taking a profit and increasing the chance of waste. The produce itself is often shipped long distances at great expense. Truck gardens raising fruits and vegetables, within one or two hours of metropolitan areas, are a thing of the past, along with the good fresh produce they used to supply.

At the opposite end of the spectrum, in countries that are just embarking on development, small farmers have converted from garden crops for their own use to cash crops which they export. Not only does this practice impoverish the soil, and in bad years the farmers, but it also impoverishes the local diet. As rural people put all their land and effort into cash crops, they are forced to import canned goods at great cost and, all too frequently, of poor nutritional quality.

Deterioration of nutritional standards due to development has been documented by the Women's Unit of the United Nations Economic Commission for Africa. Traditionally in Africa, labor was divided: men cleared the bush and women planted and maintained a garden to supply the family's vegetables. But several things happened as development began. In some cases the ablebodied men left the villages to work in the modern sector, leaving fewer people who had the physical stamina to clear the bush for gardens.

In other cases, men have been trained to use modern agricultural methods to grow cash crops and they use all their land for this purpose. This not only leaves the family without a garden plot, but also leaves the women with little to do. Even more ironically, in the parallel training programs for women, nutrition and home management classes are scheduled that have little or no, or even a contradictory, message to that in the men's classes on agricultural methods. Dichotomizing the system and the sex roles in order to promote development can have the counterintuitive result of impeding it.

Even in urban areas, care should be taken not to cause additional nutritional deterioration when replanning settlements. For example, in the very dense squatter settlements in Manila, many families keep pigs, which provide them with a potential source of capital or protein. (Fig. 5) If zoning were implemented forbidding pigs, then an alternative means of achieving the same nutritional and monetary value would have to be found.

If new technologies and new ways of thinking do not disrupt an entire way of life, they can improve the nutrition, sanitation, and health of poor families. But they must be carefully worked out so that they don't just substitute one set of problems for another.

Balwant Saini and George Chan have worked out a system of innovations in food production and waste disposal for a Pacific atoll. They did not modernize the island in the usual sense by utilizing industrial products; they improved the everyday life by applying methodologies to utilize the existing resources for increased productivity. For example, methane gas for the household cooking is produced from animal and human waste decomposition. However, the authors also have made it clear to the islanders that these developments do not necessarily reflect any long-range equilibria. They have selected available technologies for immediate application; the islanders and other consultants may well choose other technologies for incorporation into the island ecosystem at a later date. As Margaret Mead has often pointed out, peoples living in remote places not yet introduced to twentieth century technology have the opportunity of selecting their own menu from the smorgasbord of innovations available.

But only a few peoples have this chance. Most of the world's population have already been influenced by the twentieth century. More and more are choosing to leave the rural areas, where many of their needs have been fulfilled without exchange of money, in order to find paying jobs in the city. For

Fig. 5. Pigs provide families with a potential source of capital and protein

these millions, there is the possible tragedy of starvation, if only
current food production systems are used. New and more
intensive methods are needed to produce more protein, such as
Taylor Pryor's "systemculture," which yields 50 times the
average production of protein per unit of land.

Water

Only 30 percent of the world's population has access to piped
water. The rest of the world relies on wells, rivers, and other
sources that are open to contamination by pathogenic
organisms. Where there is no water, there is no life; where
there is contaminated water, there is a short life expectancy and
a high incidence of disease and suffering.

Squatter settlements, in particular, are seldom serviced
with water, and even less often with sewers. The scene of
adjacent open sewers and patched illegal water supply pipes is
common in marginal settlements (Fig. 6). In such environments
keeping clean, disposing of waste, and getting water become
major preoccupations, time consumers, and budget items. While
it is unrealistic to plan for water and sewers for everyone in all
urban areas, conditions can be improved. Alvaro Ortega has
collected a number of ideas that are applicable immediately.

Agriculture is also thirsty for fresh water. Much of the
world's arable land is already in agricultural use; in extending
cultivation into arid lands, irrigation that uses water extensively
has been found not only wasteful, but detrimental to long-run
productivity. Both Alvaro Ortega and Benjamin Zur show ways
of using water wisely with alternative water management
methods that eliminate needless consumption and permit
recycling of this not unlimited resource.

Solar Energy

There are three basic translations of solar energy: into heat,
work, and electricity. The conversion into heat is the simplest
application and its use in the near future could help all countries save fuel and increase the potential for satisfying basic
human needs. In the long run, it is the cheapest solution for

Fig. 6. Open sewer and "self-built" water-supply system, Tondo
Foreshore, Manila, the Philippines

heating. Applying scientific knowledge to reduce costs and increase efficiency of the basic equipment would create investments that would pay off not in GNP but in GNW—gross national welfare. Unlike conventional home-heating devices that often put the family at the mercy of the merchants of fossil fuels—with the expenditure accounted for in the GNP—installation of solar heat means that people can enjoy warm houses without the worries of increasingly high bills for fossil fuels. It will be hard to measure, but it would result in enabling more people to use their time to improve the human condition.

Unlike the other articles that have dealt with less privileged societies, the article on solar heating relates to its application for middle-class US families. It underlines the point that everything is in great flux: the people in America cannot go on draining the energies of the earth to heat their houses. Professor Morrison, in showing that the US house with all its electrical gadgets can be run on solar energy, therefore makes it clear that simpler houses in other parts of this world could also derive their energy needs from the sun.

All these articles illustrate human inventiveness. Each one shows new avenues that can lead to a promising twenty-first century. While there are limits to our natural resources (and limits to growth based on these) there are no limits on human ingenuity.

Recycling in Human Settlements

GEOFFREY STANFORD

To me as a physician cities are essentially insane. They breed insanity. The places we live in today must breed neurotics and psychotics. In windowless, air-conditioned rooms people cannot tell what the weather is. They do not know how their food supply is progressing. They cannot see it growing. The poor, or very poor, cannot go out and pick a berry, put it in their mouths, or see it on the shop floor, pick it up and eat it.

For nine-tenths of the evolutionary life of mankind, people have wandered out, picked what they could find and eaten it. About three hours a day was enough to feed themselves, and the rest of the time could be used to think productively and become "civilized."

This is a very real separation from our primeval self. Although each person thinks of himself as having a 50-, 60-, or 70-year life span, we carry within us our collective evolutionary life of three million years, and the imperatives that we follow naturally are certainly those of three million years. If you like to think of agriculture as being 16,000 to 17,000 years old, that is only two days in our evolutionary life span. We are thus very young as a civilized grouping and any planning for the future must take note of our evolutionary heritage.

Cities Planned with Biological Rhythms

We should design our cities so that we have biological rhythms available—the seasons, the daily rhythms. All rooms should have windows, sleep should be allowed to be longer during the winter than during the summer. All these kinds of basic facts should exist in our new planned city. Nevertheless, when we design so that people can live with the evolutionary heritage of country reality, there is no reason why they should have to abandon any of the other good "civilized" things we have acquired during the last few minutes of our total life existence as a human species.

Waste Production

If we look at ourselves, we realize that we are multiplying fast; soon we shall all be living in aggregations. People have by-products, which at present are called wastes, but which in fact are resources. These will be concentrated to much the same extent as the people producing them, so that any emerging nation will face, inevitably, the problems that are facing industrialized countries today: our waste products are embarrassingly large in volume and in concentration. We know the generation of waste in our society rises with income level. This is a straight-line curve; it is not inevitable and it may regress, but right now and for a decade or more to come it will probably increase. We now produce about three to five pounds a day per person in cities, and maybe eight to ten pounds in a highly sophisticated place like a hospital. Out in the country the farmers produce one to two pounds per person per day in their homes. One of the things we must do in planning any new settlement is to manage our wastes in advance.

Garbage is Gold

Refuse, sludge (wet and dry), and green water are being thrown away in our cities even though they can produce huge crops when applied to agricultural land: garbage is gold. We cannot afford to throw it away. This golden resource can be used by passing treated waters into lagoons for algal and fungal growth for a direct food supply or for fish for eating. The crops go either to ourselves or to animals. Animals excrete back into the sewage works; this is one cycle. Waste with or without sludge can be applied to crop land or a forest. The forest floor takes out the goodies, filters and purifies the water. The water flows down to our lakes and gives us boating, fishing, recreational, and drinking waters.

Another system is necessary for most urban trash. Solid wastes are shredded. After shredding all materials are separated. On a wet pathway, all are mixed with the sewage stream. Plastic and wood come to the surface and are skimmed off. The fats, which are high in energy content, are recovered and made into soap or margarine or burned for fuel; the plastic and wood then go back into the machine and are pulverized. Metals and other inert matter sink to the bottom. They are pushed out with a bulldozer, washed down with clean stored water, and then put back in circulation. The iron is recycled at once; the light metals are left in reserve for collection, when enough have accumulated. Paper and other biodegradables are left as a slurry in the middle, in roughly a ten-to-one ratio for most cities, as compared with solid contents in sewage. So back into the sewage works at the input end to make a thicker slurry and get a more efficient sewage works running, because the solid content is higher. Then it all goes into the stream of slurry back onto the land.

Planning Waste Management

How do we do this? We can start with the first planning for a small town. All the wastes from a new town are already planned to go ten miles to a waste recovery center. Around this center there are ten miles of good land available for spreading the recovered waste for the production of different kinds of crops. When its town reaches five thousand people, we build another one for five thousand with ten square miles for its wastes and food supply. The system of towns can be repeated and repeated, and the recovery center expanded for each. As it builds up, the waste stream becomes important. The large land crop soon needs canneries, freezers, and slaughterhouses. The surplus can be exported: the 'wastes' treatment plant' has become an agro-industry complex. Very economically, all the wastes from the food-processing plants, instead of being distributed in gutters on the road, are going right back into the main system and instantly redistributed to the land. Hence at the end there is a good system for cheap and easy management of food supply processing under modern conditions, although at the start the conditions were primitive, based on consumption by the local market.

The town relates to the rhythms of agriculture: school children can be available for setting potatoes, or cherry or strawberry picking, or whatever. The children have school holidays in season and thus are back in cycle with the seasons of the year. The social system can be in tune with the land, without destroying our city life.

Eventually a full city could be developed covering about 20 by 40 miles, depending on terrain and weather. There are banks, mosques, public libraries, cinemas and suchlike, universities, hospitals, and connective communications. It is a city of something like 100,000 people, in balance with its land supply; there are about 7 acres per person, which allows 2–5 acres for food supply, 2 acres for forestry, and plenty left over for water reserves, communications lanes, dwellings, and wild space.

We are back where we came from; these people are all seeing the seasons come and go and they are harvesting their own crops. So very roughly there is an energy balance, and an exportable surplus.

A forest of roughly ten square miles can act as the energy source for the town. Running on sunlight and the residues, it will supply enough timber to fuel a 1,000-megawatt station continuously; this is enough to supply the electrical energy for the entire system. Of course, recreational activities, forestry, and wild creatures will exist in this forest area, its water cleansing and fueling functions will continue, and the presence of the forest will provide the added benefit of stimulating rainfall.

The people are then back in touch with their evolutionary past; they are in balance with the land volume. But we know that new communities growing fast, low down in the eco-succession, are materials-hungry. They respond very quickly to a little material input, and they are gathering materials all the time. But they are quickly knocked out by abuses or by untoward environmental circumstances. When the community has progressed to a high level in the eco-succession, it has gathered a large material reserve; it changes from a material-gathering or acquisitive society, to a detritus society. It converts to a recycling, mature eco-system. We must now inform our public that we have behaved far too long as an acquisitive young society, and it is time now to grow up and become a mature, recycling society.

Now that our resources are becoming depleted—metals, timber, water, soil fertility—further production depends in large measure on returning and recycling products after using them. In other words, we process materials and pass them out into the system, and then get them back in the future, with a time lag in between. The pump that primes this system is the sun, and it is our first task to make this evident to all. If you can't recognize that, and if your projections or proposals don't fit in with that picture, then your concept is likely to be invalid; your proposal may offer the prospect of being a short-term solution, but it is likely to make another, long-term, problem. Our task is to plan, not just to solve our own immediate pressing problem, but to secure a future for our grandchildren. If we keep that goal in mind, then our solutions to today's problems become easier to identify, and the results more successful.

Integrated Farming System and Settlement Plan for Nissan Island, Papua New Guinea

GEORGE CHAN and
BALWANT SINGH SAINI

Following the trends in most parts of the developing world there are two major factors that are known to have made the maximum impact on the physical environment of the islands in Southeast Asia and the Pacific. They are the population expansion and the crisis caused by urbanization. No doubt there are other factors that are equally important, but these two seem to be the most significant.

They have followed in the wake of changes that have taken place in the old colonial picture. The emergence of nationalism has created considerable impatience in many quarters to make these islands self-reliant by rapidly building their economies. An obvious and important result of this trend is evident in the development of mineral resources and (to an increasing degree) of tourism, both of which have focused our attention on the need for conservation of the environment with all its ecological complications.

Population figures in the islands may not look impressive against those of larger countries in Asia and Latin America, but when their size and geographic limits are considered, it is not difficult to see how fast they too are approaching a crisis. Most exhibit a high rate of growth with annual average expansion of over 2.6 percent, a rate 0.6 percent higher than the world average.

The rising populations are beginning to strain the islands' existing resources, resulting in a continual drift away from the stagnant rural economies to a few urban centers. One answer to this problem may lie not only in strengthening and improving the economies of the existing rural settlements, but also in deliberately creating or enlarging a selected group of rural service centers, somewhat on the lines of those established in remote areas of Israel. Essentially, rural areas of the islands require an ecodevelopment program that integrates plantation and agricultural production, local institutions, housing, and other sectors into all-round development projects. Such projects need economic and physical planning, as well as the conservation of natural resources.

Papua New Guinea's Program

Papua New Guinea is an emerging country with most of its population in remote rural and island territories. Achieving independence in 1975, the basic objectives of the Papua New Guinea Government closely follow those outlined by the United Nations Environment Program and the United Nations Conference on Trade and Development (UNEP/UNCTAD) in October 1974 in Mexico and set out in a document known as the Cocoyoc Declaration (on the subject of self-reliance):

It (self-reliance) implies mutual benefits from trade and cooperation and a fairer redistribution of resources satisfying the basic needs. It does mean self-confidence, reliance primarily on one's own resources, human and natural, and the capacity for autonomous goal-setting and decision-making. It excludes dependence on outside influences and powers that can be converted into political pressure. It excludes exploitative trade patterns depriving countries of their natural resources for their own development. There is obviously a scope for transfer of technology, but the thrust should be on adaptation and the generation of local technology. It implies decentralization of the world economy, and sometimes also of the national economy to enhance the sense of personal participation. But it also implies increased international cooperation for collective self-reliance. Above all, it means trust in people and nations, reliance on the capacity of people themselves to invent and generate new resources and techniques, to increase their capacity to absorb them, to put them to socially beneficial use, to take a measure of command over the economy, and to generate their own way of life.

Emphasizing the need for a new approach to development styles, the Declaration calls for

Imaginative research into alternative consumption patterns, technological styles, land use strategies as well as the institutional framework and the educational requirements to sustain them. Resource-absorbing and waste-creating overconsumption should be restrained while production of essentials for the poorest sections of the population is stepped up. Low waste and clean technologies should replace the environmentally disruptive ones. More harmonious networks of human settlements could be evolved to avoid further congestion of metropolitan areas and marginalization of the countryside. In many developing countries the new development styles could imply a much more rational use of the available labor force to implement programs aimed at the conservation of natural resources, enhancement of environment, creation of the necessary infrastructure and services to grow more food as well as the strengthening of domestic industrial capacity to turn out commodities satisfying basic needs.

The Government of Papua New Guinea drew up its own set of principles in an Eight-Point Improvement Plan (shown below) which is based on equality, self-reliance, and rural development. Essentially it aims at increasing the control of economy by Papuans and New Guineans, and achieving more equality in the distribution of economic benefits and services throughout the nation. It means revitalization and improvement of the rural areas where 90 percent of the people live and work. The main emphasis is to develop a self-reliant economy, one less dependent for its needs on imported goods and services, and better able to meet the needs of its people through local production.

Eight-Point Improvement Objectives
(Approved by the Papua New Guinea Government
on 14 December 1972 for the
Second National Improvement Plan)

1. A rapid increase in the proportion of the economy under the control of Papua New Guinean individuals and groups, and in the proportion of personal and property income that goes to Papua New Guineans.
2. More equal distribution of economic benefits, including movement toward equalization of income among people and toward equalization of services among different areas of the country.
3. Decentralization of economic activity, planning, and government spending, with emphasis on agricultural development, village industry, better internal trade, and more spending channeled through local and area bodies.
4. An emphasis on small-scale artisan, service, and business activity, relying where possible on typically Papua New Guinean forms of organization.
5. A more self-reliant economy, less dependent for its needs on imported goods and services and better able to meet the needs of its people through local production.
6. An increasing capacity for meeting government spending needs from locally raised revenue.

7. A rapid increase in active and equal participation of women in all types of economic and social activity.

8. Government control and involvement in those sectors of the economy where control is necessary to assure the desired kind of development.

Eco Plan for Nissan Island

We applied these principles in drawing up a plan for Nissan Island.

Nissan, which was completely overrun, first by the Japanese and then by the US Defense Forces during the Second World War, is still fairly isolated from the rest of the world. (Fig. 7) It is approximately 30 square miles in area. Most of the four thousand people in its dozen-odd villages are primarily dependent upon coconuts, taro, sweet potatoes, and bananas as well as fish, oysters, prawns, and crayfish. (Fig. 8)

Nissan not only epitomizes the problems of dangerous decades ahead of people of the Pacific region, but indeed has relevant implications for the whole world. In a miniature and simple form this island highlights a global problem faced by all mankind: populations are increasing at an enormous speed and limited resources are likely to dictate the extent to which we can grow.

Our plan is based on the concept of the Integrated System of Farming (IFS) developed by George Chan during the last few years. It involves utilization of sun, sea, sand, sewerage, sludge, and sanitation for water supply, waste disposal and water-pollution control. There is also a proposal to produce gas for cooking, algae for animal feed, fish, and vegetables and to use the sun to produce low-cost energy for lighting, cooking, hot water, and even refrigeration. (Fig. 9)

The essential approach is to recycle everything from waste to garbage, using the sun as the only external source of energy to produce animal feed, fertilizer, and food at very little cost, with the least amount of effort, and without polluting the area— soil or sea.

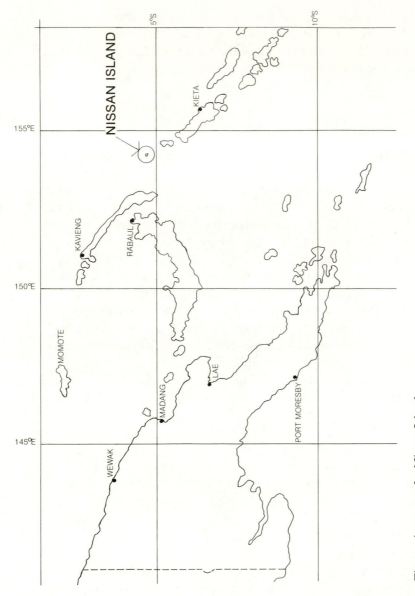

Fig. 7. Area map for Nissan Island

Fig. 8. Man of Nissan with some island foodstuffs

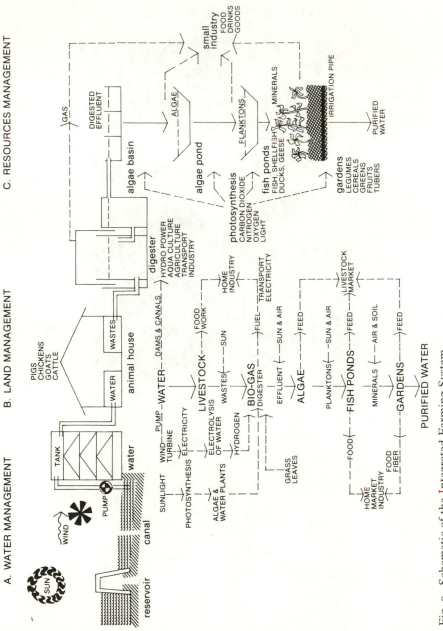

Fig. 9. Schematic of the Integrated Farming System

Water Supply

Fresh water is limited to rainwater and this can be collected only during the rainy season. Since both roof catchment and storage tanks are usually inadequate, contain impurities such as rat droppings, dead insects, leaves and dust, and can be a breeding place for mosquitos, it is important to consider alternative sources.

Groundwater above mean sea level is practically fresh, although the salinity increases with depth. Shallow wells with waterproof bottoms and infiltration galleries are practical. Water can be distilled from the sea by means of a solar still consisting of little more than a plastic-lined shallow basin with glass covers, using the sun as the source of energy.

Water Disposal

There is no such thing as waste: only people who do not know how to make use of human and animal excreta, food remains, and garbage in a scientific and sanitary manner. When these are left to rot they are not only "wastes" but also nuisances and health hazards.

An integrated system isolates human and animal excreta for reuse. Latrines and animal pens are flushed into a digester. (Figs. 10, 11) The digester allows retention of the wastes for 24 hours under quiescent, anaerobic conditions. About 69 percent of the suspended solids will settle, and decomposition of the organic matter by bacteria will reduce the volume and change its characteristics considerably.

Gases are formed (60 to 70 percent methane), and can be stored if a gas cover with a water and oil seal is fitted to the digester. Painting the gas cover black allows the maximum solar energy to be absorbed and heat the anaerobic liquid inside to activate the digestion. At the same time, pathogenic organisms are mostly destroyed.

The only way the digester can function properly is to discharge a fresh load of waste into it every day. This means that the scheme can work only if pig and/or chicken farming is

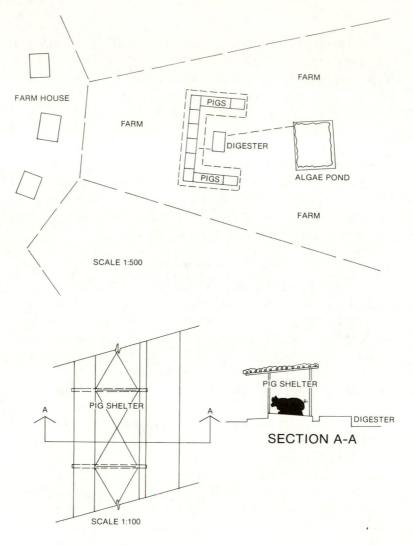

Fig. 10. Schematic of water-disposal system

done to provide the wastes which, together with natural bacteria, natural plant life, and the elements in the air (oxygen, nitrogen, and carbon dioxide), are the raw materials for the system. The pig pen and the chicken house should have a concrete floor and a plastic drain, respectively, so that the wastes can be easily washed into the digester. The possible objection by the traditional farmer to fencing in the animals is that he will have to find or buy feed for them. This objection is answered, as feed is produced at little or no cost in the same scheme.

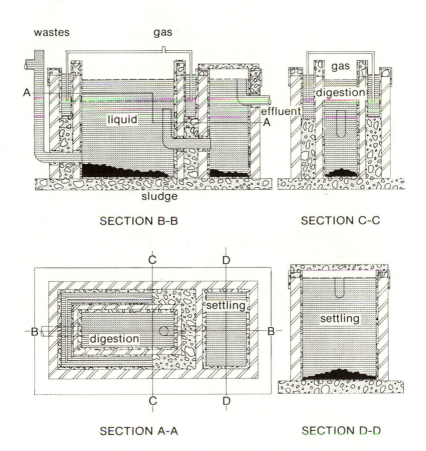

Fig. 11. Detail of digester in water-disposal system

Like any other domestic gas, methane should be treated with due respect. When it burns, it combines with oxygen to form carbon dioxide, which should be allowed to escape to the open air. For intermittent use, as in cooking and boiling water, the gas can be used directly. But for continuous use, as in refrigeration or even lighting, it is better to use the gas to run an electric generator outside the building.

It is perhaps worth noting that the digester gas, with as high as 30 percent carbon dioxide, is safer than ordinary town gas which contains 9 percent carbon monoxide. But we should always remember that air containing between 5 and 15 percent methane is explosive; there should be no naked flame when any repair is being made to the digester.

A digester of 300-gallon capacity (costing about $300) is adequate for 25 to 30 pigs and the same number of chickens, and will produce enough fuel to meet the needs of an average family. One of 50-gallon capacity, costing about $60 to $70 can cater for 5 to 10 pigs, and produce gas for cooking purposes only. The advantage of this system is that the year-round production of gas will end the need to collect hard-to-find firewood or to import expensive kerosene.

Since we intend to use the end products of our treatment system for other useful purposes, it is worth having an extension to the digester to retain the effluent for another 24 hours in a tank or pipe. More settling will take place, with further digestion by anaerobic bacteria and destruction of pathogens (bacteria, helminths, viruses). A better effluent is also obtained for subsequent purification by oxygen. This is important, because the lower number of germs and the longer retention period increase the efficiency of germ removal.

Animal Feed

The main objection from the islanders to fencing in their animals is that they have to find or buy feed, so they prefer to let their pigs and chickens roam and forage freely. (Figs. 12 and 13) As a result, the animals are underfed and produce less meat and fewer eggs.

Fig. 12. Free-foraging animals

Fig. 13. Penned, well-fed animals

The effluent from the digester is used to grow animal feed.
Algal growth is encouraged by discharging the effluent from the
settling tank into long, shallow channels, formed in a **V** -shape,
with a depth of not more than 3 feet to allow sunlight to
penetrate down to the bottom, and lined with puddle clay, or
in a rectangular shape about 12 inches deep built of concrete.
(Fig. 14)

The algae, particularly the blue-green type, are a good
source of protein and vitamins that can be used to enrich animal
feed. As a result, the animals will grow and breed faster, thus
increasing the meat supply.

It is worth pointing out that the algae are *not* part of the
original waste, but a simple natural plant that can, in the
presence of sunlight, change carbon dioxide from the air or
water into food by a biochemical process known as photosynthesis. This type of feeding is totally different from what can
be seen in some places where pigs feed on raw human excreta

Fig. 14. Settling tanks

or even on their own; or what is done on a large scale in highly developed countries where animal excrement and chemicals such as urea are mixed with animal feed to supplement the protein content.

The oxygen produced during the fixing of carbon dioxide by the algae not only purifies the effluent by converting the organic matter into minerals, but also kills the pathogens that have come out of the digester and settling tank unharmed.

Fish Culture

The effluent from the algae ponds contains nutrients that can be used in fish culture, particularly for tilapia and carp that grow and reproduce well. Fish is another source of minerals and of protein for animal feed. Provided that the pigs are not fed with fish two weeks before they are slaughtered, the pork will not have a fishy taste that may be objectionable to consumers.

As they feed on algae and protozoa, not excreta, such fish would be perfectly safe for human consumption. In any case, any enteric microorganisms will long since have been killed by the digestion and oxidation processes. Fish from the effluent ponds of this nature would be safer than several species which feed on raw sewage from sea outfalls in many parts of the world, or which are toxic, and are available in markets.

It has been found that ducks kept enclosed within the fishpond will not compete for food with the fish, but will eat what the fish do not want, thus helping to keep the pond clean. Between them they also keep mosquito larvae and weeds under control.

Shellfish can be collected from the shore when they are small, placed in plastic tubes 4 to 5 inches in diameter, and the purified effluent from the algae or fish pond circulated through them by means of a small pump, thus supplying algae and oxygen to the shellfish. If a short length of tube is replaced by some transparent material, it is possible to watch the shellfish grow.

If the same effluent is circulated in tanks in which seed

oysters are placed, the oysters will grow fat and succulent. Perhaps it should be pointed out that there is far less fear of contamination in this system than exists in the present growing of oysters and other shellfish in open seabeds, with the increasing use of the sea as a sewer for domestic and industrial wastes.

Vegetable Gardens

The overflow from the fishponds contains the end products of the decomposition of the organic matter in the sewage; these are minerals that are suitable for use as fertilizer. The stabilized sludge at the bottom of the digester is pumped out periodically and dried in a shallow bed in the ground to kill any pathogen present, before it is used as humus to improve the physical fertility of the soil. Without the use of chemicals, except for some trace elements for certain cultures, the purified effluent of the fish ponds can make vegetable gardening a very profitable proposition.

As with the fish and duck combination, it has been found that geese enclosed in a taro patch will eat the unwelcome weeds but leave the taro alone. In this case, the geese still have to be fed other food, but they do the back-breaking work of weeding and leave the farmers free for other more pleasant or profitable occupations.

The vegetables will provide the bulk of the animal feed required in this project, but where they can be sold at a high price for human consumption it is preferable to buy the cheaper animal feed, thus providing additional income for the rural family.

Application of such a program requires the active collaboration of architects and planners, public health specialists, engineers, agriculturalists, and others; but once set up the program can easily be maintained.

Settlements

Apart from proposals for improvement of land, air, and sea-transport facilities, and upgrading of utility services generally, the planning of Nissan essentially concentrates on an integrated program of rural development based on the integrated farming system and the establishment of a town center as a focus of urban activities for the islanders as a whole.

Nissan has great existing resources. Its 30 square miles of land has a number of well developed plantations and is studded with coconut palms. A variety of agricultural crops is already grown and its miles of coastline make sea products accessible.

There is a good road system threading the island, and there is considerable possibility for improving the existing jetties, thus establishing and developing better harbor facilities. The existing airstrip could be improved and better terminal facilities provided. A number of missions have already established educational institutions and a vocational school could be set up for those who wish to develop trade and other skills. (Fig. 15)

Agriculture forms perhaps the most important basis for ecodevelopment of the people of Nissan. The most economic farm unit recommended is a cluster of eight families (or multiples thereof), each of whom could be serviced with farm land of approximately 2 to $2\frac{1}{2}$ acres. The villages are generally located either close to the beach or in areas where there is room for expansion in all directions. (Fig. 16)

In cases where existing villages have more than eight families it is possible to locate farms in an extended form with those at long distances made accessible by paths acting as rights-of-way.

It has been suggested that each farm unit service a family of six (two parents and four children). It is to include a 112-square-foot piggery for ten sows, a 150-square-foot digester, an algae basin and pond of 1,200 square feet, as well as land for a fishpond and vegetable garden. Pigs, chickens, and ducks should not be allowed to roam freely but should be fenced in and given proper nutrition and husbandry. Chickens for both meat and eggs should have proper cages; ducks should have suitable ponds.

The extensive coastline facing the lagoon and the Pacific Ocean would be a reserve belonging to the whole community. Land exceeding 25 percent slope, that is, dependent upon

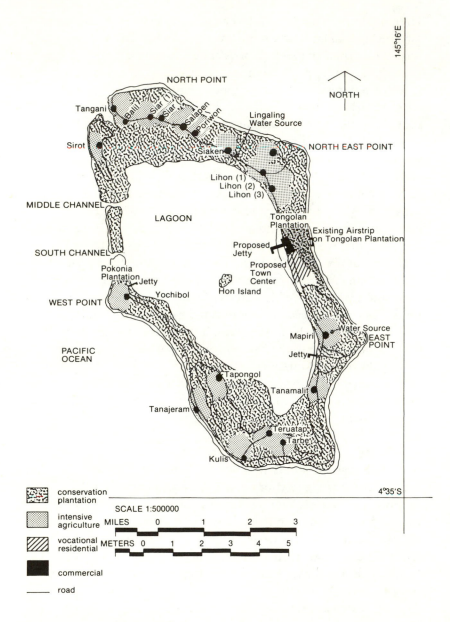

Fig. 15. Master plan for Nissan

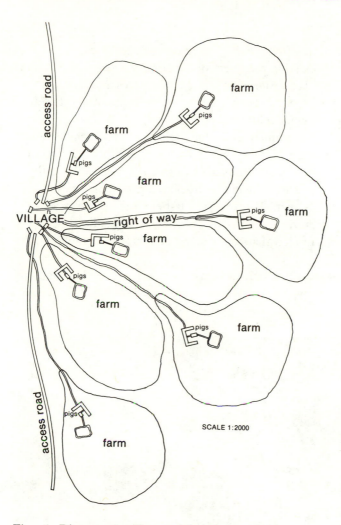

Fig. 16. Diagramatic village and farm layout

heavy vegetation to control erosion, foreshore and mangrove forests, and land unsuitable for development, such as swamps, would not be used. In addition, there are areas of special recreational, traditional, and scenic value, all of which must be carefully preserved for future generations.

Housing

The people of Nissan largely live in villages located alongside the existing road network that circles the entire Island. They have cleared ground amid coconut groves and a mixed growth of forest and coconut palms. There is abundant land for village residential development.

Our plan recommends no change in the traditional sanctioned pattern of village residential development. Inspection of existing village houses indicated to us the remarkable ability of the people of Nissan to exploit local materials and manpower, all of which has been achieved by self-help and cooperation. (Fig. 17) In our view it is important that these qualities be retained and, in fact, that active steps be taken to encourage them.

In many cases people have used scrap metal and other materials, left by the Japanese and US forces during the Second

Fig. 17. Traditional houses of Nissan, adapted to available materials

World War, as lining for walls and roofs of their houses. A number of local Catholic missions have experimented with the use of stabilized blocks made from crushing local coral and cement. Although the layout and designs of these buildings leave much to be desired, their durability and comparative maintenance-free qualities suggest their increased use in local construction.

Town Center

An island such as Nissan, with a population of some four thousand, and which is likely to increase in the foreseeable future, deserves a carefully devised program for a town center. Our plan recommends allocation of land for this purpose close to the airport and the harbor.

Apart from offering the island administrative, institutional, and commercial services, this center could also act as an exit point for island products to other parts of New Guinea. A regular farmers' market, cooperative store and a variety of small shops could be built there. The whole development will meet the needs not only of the residents but also of those who decide to live near the town center. It will complement the commercial activity of small trade stores close to the villages in other parts of the island. The services of a post office and a bank could also be made available.

As a long range project, a complex of village government council offices and a community center with associated facilities have been recommended for building on a prominent site in the town center.

Conclusion

The ecodevelopment plan endeavors to give direction to the growth of Nissan. With this growth it will be necessary to encourage individual enthusiams to improve and maintain the general appearance of the island by designing all buildings in keeping with its rural character. We have strongly recommended that no buildings on the island should be constructed higher than the nearest palm tree. We must preserve Nissan's attractive beaches from encroaching development and prevent them from becoming littered.

Most of all, a small island such as Nissan must at all costs try to keep itself free from the onslaught of tourism and preserve itself mainly for local people.

The Nissan Plan is only one of many attempts to help make people of Papua New Guinea self-reliant. Its success will lie in the way it is implemented. Knowing the qualities of the present leadership, whose own roots are firmly planted in the villages of their country, we have every confidence in the success of these proposals.

Growing Seafood on Shore

TAYLOR A. PRYOR

Two-thirds of today's protein is harvested from the ocean where most fisheries have reached their maximum potential and many are in decline. The remaining third is produced on shore, where any increase of arable land is gained at the expense of water, fuel, and natural treasures. What can be done? Between the problems of terrestrial production and the ceiling on ocean harvest, there may be one possibility which has been overlooked: the practical marriage of land and sea in order to grow seafood on land.

Traditional aquaculture, which records the highest returns of protein per hectare to date, actually contributes very little to the world protein total. For centuries it has been confined to bays and estuaries where natural spawning and local conditions allowed some modest control of growth by man. Aquaculture experts who have reviewed the worldwide activity point out that the best sites are already in use and suggest that expansion to man-made coastal sites would be done at the expense of fisheries supportive areas such as mangrove swamps. Other aquaculture enthusiasts look beyond the coast to the great blue of the ocean for bountiful future pastures, but even there are faced with such obstacles as destructive weather, predation, legal ownership, and the high costs of operation.

If such aquatic pastures could be created on shore, if those record aquatic productivity levels could be duplicated in a controlled environment, if some of the enormous organizational, financial, and technical capacity of conventional agriculture could be brought to bear on a workable system of seafood culture, then the Gordian knot of world food needs might be cut.

A commercial project capable of demonstrating this unconventional concept is well along in Hawaii. Called *systemculture*, it has been developed in steps over the last three years. The first step was an experimental unit containing oysters and clams, supplied with salt water by a swimming pool pump drawing from an ancient Hawaiian fishpond. In the course of trials over six months, the key factors of growth rate and physical management of the crop were found to be encouraging. More elaborate tests were indicated. The second step was to create a fully controlled prototype model wherein the energy required for growth of multiple crops could be quantified. In the prototype, the effluent water from an impoundment of green sea turtles was allowed to flow into several reservoirs from which the effluent then fertilized phytoplankton, a microscopic marine alga which reproduces very rapidly so that half its volume can be drained off each day as a feed for oysters. The effluent water from the oysters was then allowed to pass through a second set of reservoirs where a macroscopic alga, seaweed, was planted. The seaweed served to purge the water clean of oyster effluents and was, in turn, harvested, dried, and fed to the turtles. (Fig. 18)

The prototype farm was also supplied by an electrically driven pump, but might have been better served by a windmill with an auxiliary generator. The remainder of the energy in the system was provided from two principal sources: sunlight as absorbed by algal photosynthesis, and heat as provided by the warm tropical seawater. Seawater itself is an inorganic fertilizer and, as such, made a small energy donation.

The third step was the establishment of a demonstration farm capable of selling seafood for a profit to the Honolulu market. To do this, Oahu Oyster Farm, Inc. was formed and provided with $75,000 from the state of Hawaii's Farm Loan

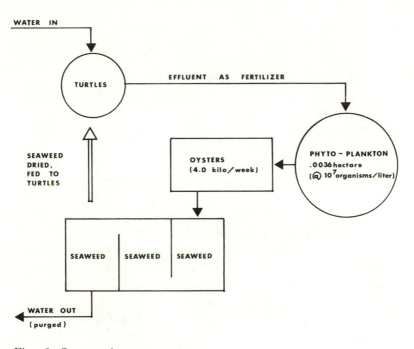

Fig. 18. Systemculture prototype

Division. Three production units were built as well as a 10,000 liter/minute wooden pump designed along the Archimedes screw principle. Again, for cost-saving purposes, a Hawaiian fishpond was utilized in lieu of the proposed phytoplankton reservoirs. Sufficient nutrients were found to be present to allow 5 metric tons of oysters a month to be harvested. The crop has a local value of $2.40 per kilo or $13,500 per month, with profits anticipated after 6 months of operations.

The final step in the development of the Hawaii project was initiated in May 1975, with the construction of a three-hectare farm. This is the first of a series of such farms planned for placement on the abandoned airfield at Kahuku, Oahu. Each hectare of diked reservoir devoted to phytoplankton culture in turn is supported by a single seafood production trench (50 m × 2.5 m) and by a set of equipment to include a windmill, a

screw-pump, and a standby generator. In addition, the three
hectare farm is equipped with a truck, a maintenance building,
a residence and custom-designed plastic pallets and trays for
management of the oysters within the production units. The
total cost of the farm is $150,000, with an equivalent amount
needed to cover operating losses until income from sales is
achieved nine months after construction begins. Production
capacity for this facility is projected at 25 metric tons/hectare/
year providing a gross revenue of $50,000/hectare/year, with
sufficient profit to repay the investment within five years.
(Fig. 19)

   In 1972 it was estimated that in the preceding 20 years the
area under irrigation throughout the world had increased nearly
threefold—from 80 million to 200 million hectares. At the same
time, the UN World Plan of Action for 1985 proposed a
"modest" gain of 600 million hectares in order to double the
1962 estimate of arable land. Accepting these estimates, it is
possible to roughly measure the merit of continuing to direct
food development resources into more and more arable lands
development, compared to the alternate of investing in aquatic
production. Since the total world production of animal protein
at the time of Andrianov's statement was estimated at 22 million
metric tons (excluding fisheries) when there were 220 million
irrigated acres cultivated, then world productivity might be
indexed at 100 kilos/hectare/year. In the Hawaii venture the
experimental results showed more than 50 tons of oysters per
hectare/year or approximately 10 tons of oyster meat, a 50:1
ratio in the world index. (These weights were derived from
algal cultures containing a density of 10^7 organisms per liter.
Densities of 10^8 are presently being maintained. This suggests
in theory a possible tenfold increase in production, to 350 metric
tons of whole oysters per hectare, 70 metric tons of oyster meat,
or around 14 metric tons of poultry if the meat is dried as feed.
In practice, only a sevenfold increase may be possible.)

   While recognizing real differences between an index of
global averages and an experimental per hectare production of
animal feed and animal protein in Hawaii, the efficiencies that

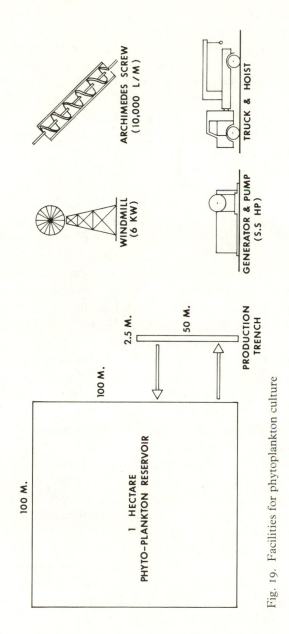

ARCHIMEDES SCREW
(10,000 L/M)

TRUCK & HOIST

WINDMILL
(6 KW)

GENERATOR & PUMP
(5.5 HP)

2.5 M.

50 M.

PRODUCTION
TRENCH

100 M.

100 M.

1 HECTARE
PHYTO-PLANKTON RESERVOIR

Fig. 19. Facilities for phytoplankton culture

seem to strongly favor aquatic production should be considered.
These are: utilization of sunlight within a column of cultured
seawater, the total utilization of fertilizers, feeds, and effluents
within an aquatic system, and the reproductive efficiency of
marine organisms, whence thousands or millions of fertilized
eggs can be drawn from a single female.

In 1971 (when world land-grown protein consumption was
at 22 million metric tons), the world fisheries harvest was
approaching 68 million tons, for a total of 90 million tons
consumed or converted to meal and oil. If the 600 million
hectares to be added by the UN plan would allow another 22
million tons of protein to be produced, nearly all of the
potential arable land would then be utilized, but available
protein will be up only 15 percent. This is because it seems
certain that the ocean harvest will remain level. If, on the other
hand, 50,000 kilos of protein per hectare/year are produced from
aquatic production, then only two million hectares are required
to actually double the total protein available. If all the production
of the aquatic acres were to be fed to swine, poultry, and even
fish, with a 10:1 conversion loss, then 20 million hectares would
be required. While large, this area still represents only one-
thirtieth of the available land needed, while providing three
times the protein of the UN plan.

To attempt to understand such a production capacity, there
are at least five factors that should be considered. First is the
physical character of the aquatic plants and animals themselves.
Supported by the water around them, they direct most of their
energy into reproduction and growth. Phytoplankton can
reproduce every eight hours; seaweed requires no stalk; oysters,
under ideal conductivity, can double their weight weekly.
Second, there is the ability of water to transport an object or
particle over great distances inexpensively, that is, without the
terrestrial costs of gravity and friction. Just as a box of cargo
can be transported from Hawaii to San Francisco cheaper than
it can be trucked from San Francisco to Los Angeles, so can a
particle of food be carried from the center of a hectare-sized
reservoir through a ditch to feed a crop and then, as a particle

of effluent, be transported back to the reservoir or off in some other direction to serve as food for another crop. When we compare the cost of passing a particle through a similar cycle on a dairy farm, we should find that the energies are one or two orders of magnitude different—the same difference we found comparing arable land and aquatic production potentials.

Third, assuming that full-scale commercial operation of systemculture in Hawaii continues to support these estimates of aquatic marine efficiencies, where does the project go from there? What locations are possible? It should first be emphasized that this is a tropical system. Just as leaving the ocean to grow seafood reverses a conventional viewpoint, so does the idea of intensive fisheries in the tropics. Occasionally biologists refer to the oceans of the Central and South Pacific as "desert," meaning that they are low in nutrients and low in life. However, such descriptions are ecologically incorrect. Certainly, where the ocean is deep and the water warm, the area will be low in nutrients since any particulate matter will eventually be consumed or will fall to the seafloor with no chance of being recycled back up the water column to the surface again. This is why the great fisheries of the world have traditionally been in the cold-water areas where the dense water and the shallow depth allow a high level of nutrients and planktonic growth in the surface waters for as deep as light can penetrate. Obviously, the compact biomass that results can be efficiently harvested under such conditions, but this is not to say that such a biomass is any greater than in the tropical oceans if measured by the same space parameter, "as deep as light can penetrate." In Hawaii the biomass spreads down to over 200 meters, whereas 20 meters is closer to the bottom limit off Alaska. Since the warmth of the water further encourages growth and does so for a full 12 months, one can estimate that the gross return of the tropical ocean is comparable to the cold regions, only harder to observe and a great deal less accessible. It is the last difficulty that has led to expert appraisal of the South Pacific, as having "poor productive potential." Now it appears that the opposite is the case, that tropical seawater, if confined to man-made shallows and if fertilized, can vastly exceed the returns of the traditional fisheries sites simply because the best assets of both regions can be combined only in the tropics. These assets are sunlight, warm water, and year-around growth. If one adds locally generated nutrients and windpower, the advantage of the tropics is very large, suggesting the potential of a controlled seafood industry where none exists today. (Fig. 20)

Fourth, aside from locating generically in the "tropics" from 22° north to 22° south latitudes, sites for systemculture should have the following features: (1) flat land with seawater available either from wells or from coastal access; (2) sunlight for at least nine months a year; (3) a temperature range at least in the mid-seventies; (4) not more than 6 meters difference in height between the water in the system and sea level; (5) wind for most of the year between 5 and 15 knots (or, alternately, nearby petroleum production); (6) a labor force capable of agricultural vocational training; and (7) some access to market if export sales rather than local consumption are planned.

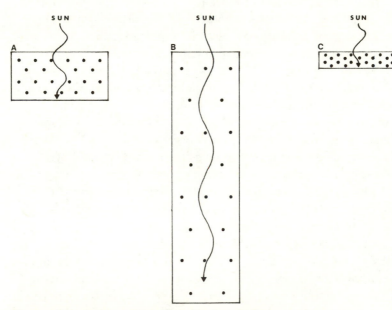

Fig. 20. Tropical seawaters, if confined to shallows, can be more productive than temperate seawaters

Fifth, systemculture has still another unconventional feature, that is, a uniform design which will allow the production of a variety of seafood crops. In fact, as was demonstrated by the prototype, the system functions best as more crops are added. Besides benefiting the internal energies, they also add a broader market base to the investment. A farm which starts with octopus, oyster, and clam production can have many harvests of each for several years while it is growing the first turtle crop and developing skills in lobster, shrimp, and fish. Once all of these crops are in full production, the ratio of one to the other on the farm can be altered depending on local preference, export markets, and operational experience within local conditions. The point is that the farm can choose from any seafood for which there is a hatchery capability.

If systemculture continues to have merit as a potential industry, it will need financing, training, and continuing technical support. In Hawaii, the next 12 hectares of farm are to be built with funds from private investors who are willing to participate as limited partners with the developer. No state or federal funds of any kind appear to be available to a new commercial aquatic venture. While the Production Credit Association allows for aquatic farming within its bylaws, it also requires a minimum of 12 months' operating experience before even accepting an application. Ordinary bank financing is several years off, while federal subsidies for production development are not even being contemplated. Outside the United States, international development banks offer a more promising picture. This promise will probably lead to a second farm, in parallel with the Hawaii venture, in the near future. Writing on the "Role of Traditional Agriculture" (*Ekistics* 230, Jan 1975), Earl Kulp gives some succinct advice on how to broadly encourage a new production technique.

Concentrate

Move the project "point, line, network." The Chinese have a saying that every project should evolve in three stages, which translate most freely as "point, line, network." This means one should advance the project:

Point phase: Start the first year in only one or two
locations, with about ten to forty farmers in each. Senior
officials must spend a good deal of time working with the
first group of farmers, to learn what problems are
encountered and what routines work.

Line phase: In the second year expand the project to about
five to ten locations, to try the program under varying
conditions that may be found in the zone. Some prior
guidance and training can be given to the field staff, but
senior officials must still make themselves available at all
times for troubleshooting, for solving unforeseen problems.

Network phase: Once the lessons of the line phase have
been learned, expand the project as fast as resources will
allow, to blanket the zone.

Kulp encourages the production developer to resist
political pressures to start out too big or to start everywhere at
once. If one listens to the sound of experience, systemculture
should be confined to Hawaii and perhaps to the Philippines
for several years. The first location has advantages as a technical
base where hatchery skills, nutritional research, and engineering
advances can be made most rapidly in the early years. Hawaii
would also serve well as model farm and training center. It is at
the center of a well-developed local and export marketing
system and should thrive in the initial years. A site in the
Philippines might, on the other hand, lend itself to expansion
with lower costs for land, construction, and operation, and
probably encourage a much larger scale of development in the
future. Supervisors from the Philippines could be trained in
Hawaii, perhaps through the auspices of the East-West Center;
and they, in turn, could train the operating staff at home. If
export is the goal, both locations might cooperate from the first
under a single trade name and combined sales program.

In the "line" phase, the perfect program would proceed to
test other varied locations, perhaps to include an atoll, a desert,
and an urban site (for utilization of sewage). Areas might

include the Cook Islands, the west Australian desert, and Dagat-Dagatan, Manila, or Sand Island, Honolulu. In the network phase, Kulp gives license to "blanket the zone." In the Pacific, assuming that systemculture can be viable on a scale of 1 hectare to a 1,000 hectares or more, the zone would include a great many potential sites and political environments. It is possible the latter may be more limiting than the former, since new developments tend to generate their own opposition as well as enthusiasm and support.

The potential of aquatic production has been sometimes referred to as the "blue revolution." It may well prove to be an apt expression even though cultured reservoir water appears green to nonpoets. Aquatic production has the additional merit of being able to utilize renewable resources such as wind, sun, and seawater. It is nonpolluting, since it can fully utilize all nutrients and feed internally. It offers a high quality type labor. Systemculture lends itself to operation in conjunction with other compatible systems such as controlled environment greenhouses, with dirigible transportation systems that can provide high payload, low-cost cargo hauls along distant coastlines or between island communities, and it is compatible with sewage disposal systems as it can provide for full utilization of animal or human waste. Systemculture offers the option of small, medium, or large scale, or local consumption or export, of being centralized industrially or decentralized for rural development and even of slow step-by-step improvement or rapid slam-bang "feed the world" expansion. Finally, the crops that it produces offer the greatest boon of all; they taste good.

When the above was presented to the participants in March 1975 to a Regional Human Settlements Workshop in the Philippines, sponsored by the United Nations and the Development Academy of the Philippines, one of the many questions that followed was "what is needed to get it moving?" The response was an age-old one: money. Funds for point, line, and network planning, funds for maximizing the information to be extracted from model farms, funds for hatchery progress in more crops, funds for training. Beyond these, there is a need

for ordinary capital improvement loans and for crop loans to
carry the farms through to the first sales. Granted that there is
a world food gap approaching and granted that the aquatic
potential could possibly fill that gap, why not divert some small
part of the total funding designated now for agriculture towards
growing seafood on land? Why not try a blue revolution?

Simple Water Technologies

ALVARO ORTEGA

I n many parts of the world there is water, but it is saline, brackish, or polluted, and consequently unsuitable for drinking. The solution of this problem would open up many areas that have been considered uninhabitable. Inexpensive water purification based on the abundant solar energy found in many tropical areas can change this factor. A solar still for each dwelling using simple technology and local materials, would lend itself to immediate application in many parts of the world with low initial investment and minimal operating cost.

Figure 21 illustrates a still that uses solar radiation to evaporate the saline water in the basin, then condenses the resulting water vapors on the underside of the sloped cover and collects the distilled water in troughs on either side. Each square meter of still can produce three to four liters of potable water a day, depending on the hours of sunshine in that locality. The minimum physiological requirements for water per person per day is two liters.

Production of Groundwater

In places where there is a minimal amount of groundwater or rainfall, the only possible sources of water are in the ground moisture and in the atmosphere itself. Depending on soil

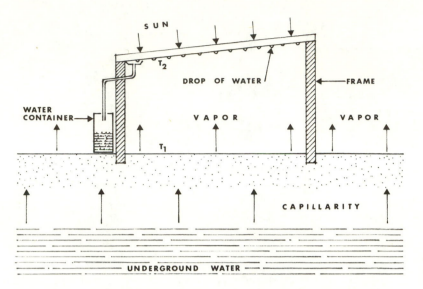

Fig. 21. In Japan and Pakistan moisture is drawn out of the ground
and collected. Such systems supply only minimal amounts of water

conditions, ground moisture can yield small quantities of water.
When the ground surface is heated by the sun, the water vapor
is raised by capillarity, and this moisture can be collected in the
form of droplets. Figure 22 shows the method developed by
Japan and Pakistan.

Production of Water from the Atmosphere

The air surrounding the earth contains large quantities of water
in vapor form. The amount varies from place to place. Air over
tropical areas contains more moisture than air over colder land.
The amount of water vapor the air can hold depends on the
temperature: the higher the temperature the more vapor; the
lower, the less vapor, and so the moisture condenses into water
droplets.

Under certain relative humidity and temperature conditions,
the moisture in the air can be abstracted and made available for
human use. It is necessary to rely on specific prevailing wind,
moisture, and temperature conditions.

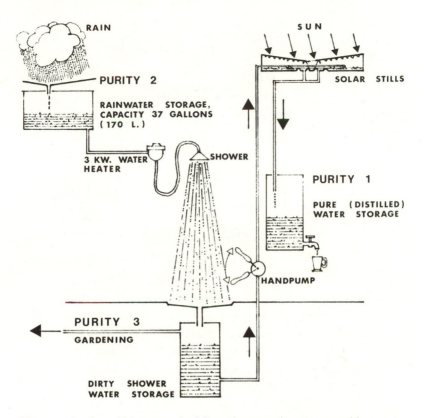

Fig. 22. A solar still integrated with a rainwater cistern to provide household water system

In ancient Theodosia, Crimea, heaps of stones 25 to 30 meters across, and 10 meters high were built to create artificial atmospheric springs (Figure 23). The circulation of warm moist air produced by the prevailing wind in contact with this pile, where the inside temperature was much lower than the air temperature, caused condensation; this water was collected to form the water supply for the city.

There are also natural atmospheric springs such as those of Henne-Morte in Haute Garonne in France. The very low temperature of these caverns combines with moist warm air

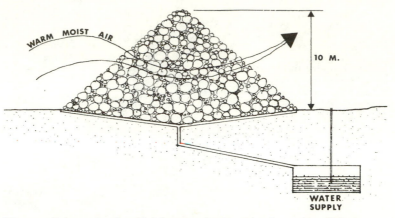

Fig. 23. Schematic of artificial atmospheric spring in ancient Crimea

circulating through them to cause condensation on the walls and a resulting supply of water.

On the island of Lanzarote (Canaries) tomato growers place a layer of fine black volcanic sand around their plants. During the night, this sand cools through radiation and condenses the airborne water, which by gravity drops down and waters the roots of the plants. Similarly, in the past in Israel, heaps of stones were placed around the bases of trees in desert plantations.

Conservation of Water

In a modern bathroom about 5 liters of water are used to wash one's hands, 20 liters to flush a toilet, 100 liters to take a shower, and 300 liters to fill a bathtub.

But 70 percent of the world's population do not have modern bathrooms and piped-in water. They must carry their water, frequently from a considerable distance. The minimum amount of water required per person per day for washing and cooking is 20 liters, weighing 20 kilograms. Considerable energy and caloric output per person can be expended in carrying 20 kilograms of water each day for each member of the family.

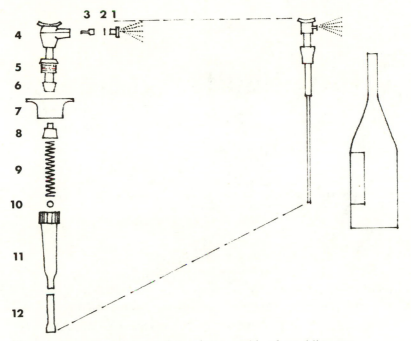

Fig. 24. An easily constructed atomizer, capable of providing one hundred hand washings from one liter of water

The amount of water required for washing can be reduced by using spray or atomizer equipment. With an efficient atomi-atomizer, one liter of water is sufficient for one hundred hand-washings. This is a significant saving, and may also result in better hygiene by offering an opportunity to keep clean even in locations that lack a convenient water supply. (Fig. 24)

Controlled Irrigation

BENJAMIN ZUR

ater is a major environmental variable in increasing food production. The dependence on water of both growth and the eventual yield of crops, stems from the sensitivity of most vegetative and reproductive plant processes to the level of water deficit developed in the crop. Water deficits develop in plants as a result of the lag in water absorption by the roots behind the transpirational water loss by the leaves.

In plants growing in soil, water absorption by the roots results in a gradual drying of the surrounding soil. As the soil dries, it becomes increasingly difficult and eventually impossible for the root system to maintain water absorption at a rate equal to the transpirational flux. Thus, as time advances, the water deficit in the crop gradually increases. Recent research on the sensitivity of plants to the level of the water deficit showed that the growth of most agricultural crops is extremely sensitive to even slight water deficits.

Effect of Irrigation

Following proper irrigation, the soil surrounding the root system is rewetted, the water uptake rate increases, and the water deficit that had developed in the plant since the last irrigation is dissipated. The amount of water required for a proper irrigation cannot be chosen at will. It depends on the depth or volume of the root zone and the storage capacity of the soil. Larger amounts of water will simply wet a greater depth and vice versa. Even when leaching of soluble salts is required, the leaching depth must be specified. Based on these simple considerations, we conclude as follows:

The objective of irrigation is to control the level of the crop water deficit in order to obtain the most economical yield.

The time interval between irrigations is a basic tool to control the level of water deficit in the crop.

Irrigation should result in the rewetting of the soil in the root zone so that water uptake by the roots can proceed unimpeded.

The amount of water applied at each irrigation is a fixed quantity determined by the depth or volume of the root zone and the storage capacity of the soil.

Plant roots require sufficient oxygen flux in order to carry out their basic functions. The ability of roots to grow, absorb water, and take up nutrients is seriously impeded as a result of oxygen deficiency. Oxygen is supplied to the roots through the soil by diffusion which can take place only if the soil pores are water free. Oxygen diffusion through wet soil will proceed only above a certain threshold value of water-free porosity—approximately ten percent for most soils and crops.

The oxygen needs of plant roots interfere with their water requirements. To maintain unimpeded water flux, a water-saturated soil would be ideal, since the resistance to water flow is minimal. However, oxygen diffusion is inhibited under these conditions and plant growth would therefore be restricted. Thus, the water-air relationship in the soil must be controlled so that the soil is never wetted above a maximal water content.

The maximal water content of the soil must prevent oxygen deficiencies in the root zone. The minimal water content should prevent the development of undesirable water deficits in the crop. The depth or volume of the wetted soil should ensure

optimal water and oxygen throughout the root zone and an extra
depth or volume when leaching of soluble salts is needed.

Limitations of Conventional Irrigation

Conventional irrigation methods result in excess wetting of the
soil during irrigation. Following irrigation, the excess water
drains downward to wet an additional depth. When the drainage
essentially ceases, the whole wetted depth is at a water content
level termed field capacity. During the irrigation and part of the
drainage stage, the upper part of the soil profile is too wet to
allow free oxygen supply to the roots. The cumulative damage to
the crop due to oxygen deficiency in the root zone depends on
the irrigation interval. The shorter the irrigation interval, the
longer the cumulative time the root system is deficient in oxygen
and the larger the damage to the crop. This is probably one
reason why irrigation can result in a reduction in crop yields.

New Irrigation Methods

The Technion Soils Laboratory has made a major effort to
develop irrigation methods capable of controlling soil water
content during wetting. The water content of the soil profile
during infiltration depends to a large degree on the water
application rate, when the application rate is smaller than the
infiltration capacity of the soil. In order to wet the soil directly
to water contents which do not restrict oxygen diffusion, application rates in the range of 0.5 to 2.0 millimeters per hour must
be applied. No available sprinkler or dripper can apply water at
such low rates. Accordingly, two irrigation methods were
developed: pulsed sprinkler or dripper irrigation, and porous
tube irrigation.

The pulsed water application method was developed in
order to reduce the water application rate of existing sprinklers
or drippers. By operating a sprinkler or a dripper in a pulsed
manner, its average application rate is lower than its nominal
application rate. Both theoretical and experimental research into
the water distribution in a soil by this system have shown that
the water content in the soil profile is determined by the time-

averaged application rate. This was generally true provided the nominal application rate was not too high.

The technological advantage of the pulsed irrigation principle is that it can be used with available sprinklers, drippers, or any kind of water emitter. What is required is a control unit that can open and shut at predetermined pulse durations and intervals. Completely automated hydraulic and electronic control units were developed and successfully field tested in our laboratory.

Porous tube irrigation was developed in order to obtain a controlled wetting of the soil volume surrounding the porous tube. The water application rate in a two-dimensional geometry such as exists around a porous tube is equal to the flux per unit length of the porous tube, divided by the wetted periphery.

Thus the water application rate around a porous tube is not a constant, but is inversely proportional to the radial distance away from the tube. The flux through the porous tube can therefore be predetermined so that all or most of the soil volume surrounding the tube would never be wet above a maximal oxygen-limiting water content level. A plastic porous tube developed by Hydronautics Israel was found to have the desired fluxes and was successfully tested in the field.

The overall objective of the concepts and the new irrigation methods described above is to maximize crop production through accurate control of the water variable. Such control requires frequent irrigation and in some cases even continuous irrigation. The practice of frequent irrigation is almost synonymous with wasting water, or at least using larger than normal quantities of water. The approach here is not to "save" water, nor to waste it. Rather, our aim is to use the available water more efficiently, obtaining higher yield outputs for about the same water inputs.

It is now firmly established that the changes with time of the daily water loss from a crop completely covering the ground go through two stages. During the first stage, the daily water loss is constant with time and is equal to the potential evapotranspiration. The duration of this stage depends on climatic conditions, type of soil, and depth of root zone. During the second stage, the daily water loss gradually decreases. The amount of water applied at each irrigation, for irrigation intervals shorter than the duration of the constant water-loss stage, should be equal to the daily water loss multiplied by the irrigation interval. Furthermore, the cumulative water use under these conditions will be constant and independent of the irrigation interval. For irrigation intervals longer than the duration of the constant daily water-loss stage, the cumulative water use will decrease as the irrigation interval becomes longer. This is one of the major reasons for irrigation at long interals.

There are indications that within the short irrigation interval range (1 to 5 days) crop yield increases as the irrigation interval is shortened. If this irrigation interval range is within the constant daily water-loss stage, then a yield increase is obtained without any increase in the cumulative water use. The water production function is vertical and the efficiency of water use is infinite.

Daily Pulsed Irrigation of a Grapefruit Grove

This experimental grove is planted on a heavy clay soil and is normally sprinkler-irrigated once every two weeks. An extreme treatment of daily irrigation, using a completely automated pulsed sprinkler irrigation system, was initiated two years ago. The daily amounts of water applied were determined on the basis of a certain seasonally variable ratio of evaporation from a class A pan as is normally used in the area. The water pulses were repeated each hour until the daily amount of water was applied. The time-averaged water application rate was 0.7 mm/h. (Table 1)

A 25-percent increase in the number of fruits per tree and a 30-percent increase in the yield of grapefruit per tree were obtained. This was obtained with essentially the same amount of water applied in both treatments. The soil water regime, as recorded by tensimeters and frequent sampling, was found to be essentially constant, with time at a water content near field capacity. The soil profile down to a depth of 80 cm was

Table 1.   Daily Pulsed Irrigation of a Grapefruit Grove

Parameter	Daily pulsed Irrigation	Irrigation at Two-week Interval
Fruits per tree	1180	940
Average fruit wt—gm	289	272
Average yield per tree—kg	341	240
Water applied—mm^3	820	840

uniformly wet to essentially this water content before, during and after the water application. The trees looked healthy with essentially continuous new outgrowth throughout the irrigation season.

Corn Irrigation with Porous Tubes

This experiment was performed on sandy loam soil.
Daily porous tube irrigation was compared to daily drip irrigation. The corn was planted in two close rows (30 cm apart) spaced 1.80 cm between the centers of pairs. The porous tubes were buried to a depth of 15 cm between the two rows. The drippers were spaced 0.5 cm apart along the pipe which was also placed between two rows. The discharge of each dripper was 2 liters per hour while that of the porous tube was 0.9 liters per hour per meter length.

Table 2.   Corn Irrigation with Porous Tube

Parameter	Porous tube Irrigation	Drip Irrigation
No. of grade A cobs per plot	103	85
Wt. of grade A cobs—kg	31.8	26.1
Av. height—cm	190	175
Av. wt. of plants from 2 m row—kg	11.50	9.40
Total water applied—m^3	615	740

Both the yield and the vegetative development of the corn plants grown under porous tube irrigation increased by 20 percent as compared to those under the drip irrigation. These results were obtained while using 17 percent less water. Except for a short distance from the porous tube, the soil water content was essentially maintained at field capacity.

Solar Energy for Dwellings

C. A. MORRISON

Solar energy can contribute largely to reducing the demands on fossil fuel supplies. It is ideally suited to residential energy, and can be readily adapted to use in small industry. Since the amount of insolation per square meter is fixed in nature, solar energy is easiest to apply to structures one to three stories high. Some solar energy has been used in residential units throughout the world for many years. But its use has been largely restricted to specialized tasks, rather than to fulfilling all the energy requirements of a modern house. Various houses have been experimentally equipped with solar heating or cooling devices, but all the energy requirements of a standard house are available at the site if they are utilized to the greatest possible extent.

Hot Water for Household Needs

The potable hot water required for residential use can be supplied by a flat-plate solar collector, using either a single or a binary fluid system. In climates where hard freezes are unusual, a single-fluid unit can be used. In climates where it freezes

several times a year, a binary fluid system should be used, so
that the energy-collecting fluid, which remains in the exposed
solar collector during the night, will not freeze and damage the
collector components. In such a case, the fluid circulating
through the coils of the solar collector should be treated to
reduce its freezing point below the level of anticipated freezes.
The separate supply of potable water will receive its heat by
means of a suitable heat-transfer device within the storage tank.

A sketch of the solar water-heater arrangement is given in
Figure 25. It shows that the bottom of the hot-water storage
tank is located above the top of the collection unit. This
arrangement makes use of natural convection for fluid circulation
within the water heating system. If circumstances dictate that
the storage tank be located below the collector surface, a pump
is required (one-fifth horsepower is enough). While these
comments apply specifically to the arrangement shown in
Figure 28, they apply to all flat-plate solar collectors, regardless
of their arrangement and the type of equipment they use.

Residential Space Heating

House heating requirements can be met by flat-plate solar
collectors if proper storage is provided for the heated fluid,
which will then be effective during prolonged poor weather.
Before the system is designed five- to ten-year local weather
history is needed to determine the size of reservoir necessary.

Baseboard convectors, radiant panels, or conventional
radiators can be used to provide heat with a minimum need for
auxiliary energy. The heat is distributed by means of natural
convection as the cool air comes in contact with the warm heater
surfaces.

A scheme for space heating and hot-water equipment is
shown in Figure 26. The number of collectors required depends
on the floor area to be heated, the type of insulation used in the
house, the amount of infiltration expected, and other parameters
that affect heat loss. In general, one square meter of collector is
adequate for three square meters of floor space.

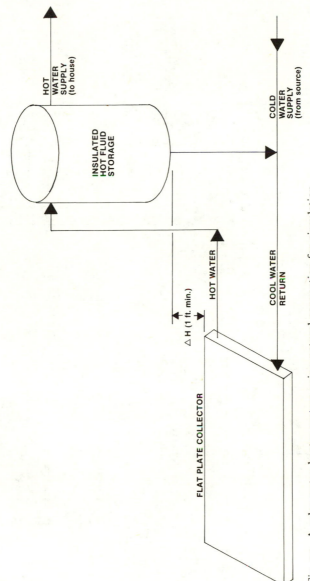

HOT
WATER
SUPPLY
(to house)

COLD
WATER
SUPPLY
(from source)

INSULATED
HOT FLUID
STORAGE

HOT WATER

COOL WATER
RETURN

△ H (1 ft. min.)

FLAT PLATE COLLECTOR

Fig. 25. A solar water-heater system using natural convection for circulation

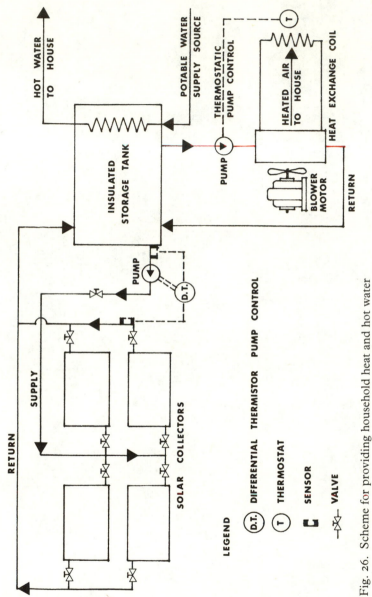

Fig. 26. Scheme for providing household heat and hot water

Operation of the System

The hot-fluid storage tank should be well insulated to minimize heat loss. The circulation pump moves the water from the storage tank through the heat exchanger coil, and the cooled water is returned to the insulated storage tank. As the blower pushes air over the heat-exchanger coil, the air is heated and circulated through the house by its normal air distribution system. The circulation pump is thermostatically controlled, and can be regulated like any standard central-heating system.

The schematic arrangement shown uses an air distribution system merely because it is easily adapted if the house is air-conditioned. If the house has a hydraulic system, the schematic arrangement will work equally well by pumping the hot fluid through the heating system. This is the arrangement used in the University of Florida test house.

Figure 27 shows one way power can be generated. Hot water is drawn from the insulated storage tank by the circulation pump and delivered to a vapor generator which contains a volatile vapor. As the refrigerant expands from liquid into high-pressure vapor, it may be used to drive a piston or other type of vapor engine, which in turn delivers power to a generator for either DC or AC electricity. The effluent from the vapor engine generator set passes into a condenser where the refrigerant is condensed by a cooling medium—water or air. The liquid from the vapor generator, the refrigerant, is revaporized and the cycle repeated. The energy required to raise the pressure is relatively small compared to the power delivered by the vapor engine generator set. Therefore, the pump can operate either off the electric energy supplied or from a properly geared mechanism designed into the vapor engine itself.

If direct current is generated, it must be transformed into alternating current, and the voltage usually must be amplified to meet the requirements of standard electrical equipment. Since it is desirable to have power adequate to meet peak electric energy demands, the generating equipment must be big enough to meet these requirements, and storage batteries can supply a reserve capacity.

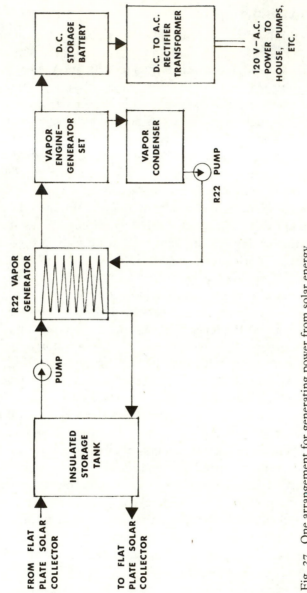

Fig. 27. One arrangement for generating power from solar energy

Solar-Powered Cooking

With solar-powered electric energy at hand, it is obvious that cooking could be done by electricity. There is an alternate method, however, which employs the high-temperature fluids directly, and is therefore a more efficient use of the energy available. Since the flat-plate collector does not generate the high temperatures required for cooking, a solar concentrator is required.

In a solar concentrator the system fluid enters at the bottom, picks up heat as it travels upward through the concentrator, and returns to the storage compartment of the system as it leaves the top portion. The reflectors on this concentrator are parabolic, to concentrate the rays of the sun on the tube containing the fluid to be heated, which lies at the focus of the parabola.

Since the solar concentrator depends on receiving the direct rays of the sun in order to heat effectively, it must be able to track the sun in order to continue concentrating solar rays on the focal point of the parabola. Providing for such a tracking device complicates the design, since the collector surface must be free to rotate continuously during the course of the day. In addition, the concentrator must track the sun as its course shifts from north to south during changes of season. This movement can be instrumented to perform automatically, but weekly manual adjustments would be quite adequate.

Because the solar concentrator is effective only when exposed to direct solar energy, a storage capacity is required to operate the cooking system during poor weather. This is diagramed in Figure 28. As the hot fluid leaves the solar concentrator, it is delivered to an insulated storage tank, and circulated either by a pump or by thermally induced circulation.

The cooking unit itself may be either a conventional stove or individual surface units with a separate oven. In either case, a manual switch must be located nearby to turn on the electric pump that circulates the hot fluid from the storage tanks to the cooking unit. The amount of heat delivered to each cooking unit is controlled by its own valve, that operates in the same manner

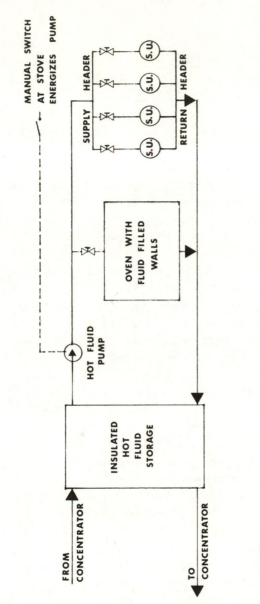

Fig. 28. Storage unit scheme for maintaining solar-powered cooking in any weather

as the control knobs on a standard electric or gas stove. The rate at which heat is delivered to the units depends on the temperature drop across these units and the rate of mass flow through the units. Since the mass flow rate can be varied from zero to maximum system capacity, a wide range of control settings is available. As the control mechanism itself is basically the same as those already in use, there should be no difficulty in making the transition from either electric or gas cooking to solar cooking.

Economics

The cost of making a house self-sufficient in terms of energy with the techniques outlined in this paper is approximately twice the cost of a conventional installation in the USA. Annual savings will more than offset the initial outlay.

PART III

Shelter and Movement

Introduction

GWEN BELL

hile the needs for better shelter and movement
are universal, they cannot be met by a single
design for a house or vehicle. Each house has to satisfy particular
cultural needs, protect the inhabitants from the vagaries of the
local weather, tie into a servicing system, and relate to areas of
employment; similarly each vehicle must be compatible with
established rights-of-way, storage places, and available energy
sources. Yet housing and transporatation problems are often
outlined on a global basis.

The great gap between defining the universal problem and
determining a local solution must be bridged. The global
concepts need to be elaborated in terms of local applications and
then generalizations may be made from local patterns.

David Aradeon presents examples of misplaced
technological improvements and local adaptations. He argues
that if the use of local materials was required, then there would
be the more appropriately scaled jeepney-like vehicles rather
than Mercedes-Benz buses, and lived-in houses rather than
vacant asbestos prefabricated shells. Such a requirement could
force the experts to *consider* the local alternative materials, but
should not force their use.

The next articles derive from the work that is being carried
out in institutions in the "rich" countries that are making serious

efforts to contribute to and coordinate with building activities throughout the world. The International Development Research Centre of Canada sponsors a number of projects and workshops on determining appropriate building systems; the Intermediate Technology Development Group in the UK acts as a task force that solves problems of developing needed, simple technologies; the Technology and Development Institute of the East-West Center in Hawaii is coordinating the activities of and disseminating information to low-cost housing technology centers throughout the Pacific region; the Centre Scientifique et Technique du Bâtiment in Paris and the German Democratic Republic Academy of Building have both been in the forefront in developing cheaper mass-produced building components.

While the large agencies are responsible for the diffusion and implementation of new ideas, the brilliant new concepts still come from individual inventors. Although Fuller's dome, Lindstrom's water-free toilet, Goicoechea's vertebrate train, and Wuellenkemper's airship are not newly invented, nevertheless, each of these inventions is truly innovative and, if widely accepted, could improve the conditions of human settlements.

Then why haven't they been utilized?

Each one, to be incorporated into an urban plan, calls for reform in the established ways of doing things. Domes do not fall under the standard building codes; water-free waste disposal systems do not fit the specifications of sanitary engineers; vertebrate trains cannot be adapted from present vehicles and guideway systems; and airships do not fit the plans of the international air-carrier corporations. There is a very strong tendency to conservatism on the part of all nations and their leaders. Implementation of any of these proposals would demand investing in an unknown, rather than gradually improving what is. Yet, there are, and must be, times for drastic change. Investment in revolutionary ideas—the Panama Canal, the Toronto subway system, the beautiful parkway along Copacabana in Rio de Janeiro, the Japanese Bullet train, the new city of Islamabad—make dramatic statements and often give new hope for the future. But at the same time, there is a need for projects that slowly improve upon everyday living conditions. This is not an easy mixture to achieve—but it is always important to consider both the evolutionary and revolutionary solutions to problems of building human settlements.

Using Local Resources

DAVID ARADEON

Picture the density of the people in an African market.
(See Fig. 29) All kinds of activities occur simultaneously: eating, cooking, vehicular movement, selling,
garbage disposal. The problems in African cities are very
different from those of the rural areas, so that the approach has
to be different. Although it might be expected that, when a man
comes into the city, he accepts the discipline the city imposes
on him, the fact remains that in cities like Lagos and Accra,
everyone operates on different time-space concepts. In Africa,
there is a diversity of levels of comfort for the individual, from
the most primitive to highly sophisticated, Western standards.
Imports still provide the basis of modernization; buses imported
from Germany must travel in narrow streets with open drains.
(Fig. 30)

Dogon Cliff Villages, Mali

The villages of the Dogon in Mali illustrate the traditional
environment. The people live on the cliffs, in a series of plazas.
The center of Dogon life is usually the funeral place, the widest
plaza in the village. During droughts the people sacrifice at the
funeral plaza to appease the gods and get water for their farms.
And if these people were to be resettled, use of such a plaza is an
important element that would need to be considered.

Fig. 29. Market day in Akosombo, Ghana (WFP/FAO photo by Peyton Johnson)

The Dogon people live in harsh terrain, and have used all the available space to build on. The granaries have been built right into the cliffs. They overcome height problems without any advantage of sophisticated technology. Their building technique is very simple. Although they use stones without mortared joints, they plaster the outside. Boulders on the hillside not only become support for the building, but sometimes become part of it. For the Dogon the granaries are important architecturally and symbolically. Storing food is a very important element of their life; the architecture is therefore dominated, especially in the Dogon area, by granaries.

There are no professional builders in the Dogon culture or in the other cultures in this area. Everybody can, and everybody does, build. Building activities are carried on when there is no farming to do. The streets in these hillside villages are not built for vehicular movement. Yet you find social activity areas, such

Fig. 30. An imported bus contrasts with open sewage drains in Lagos,
Nigeria

as places for children to play and a large pavilion where all the people get together to amuse themselves and talk.

The Displaced Gongawa and the Well-Intentioned Architect

The Bunsuru settlement was built in central Nigeria to resettle a village being displaced for the Niger dam. The architect who designed the settlement had about 25 years experience in Nigeria, and was very well aware and appreciative of the culture of the country. He tried his very best to duplicate the culture by duplicating the form of his houses. (Fig. 31) But his approach was one that could have resulted from purely looking at the old settlements from the air. The sense of scale and the idea of what constitutes the family unit were lost. The new mud houses have asbestos roofs and concrete block walls; the perforated walls are the kitchens, the non-perforated ones the dwellings. (Fig. 32) The Gongawas didn't like these houses, so they deserted them and, not far from the new settlement, built what they were used to building.

The big difference between the architecture they built and the architect's architecture was very simple. He tried to duplicate the form, but these people don't look at their architecture in terms of form, but in terms of spaces and comfort. Their traditional thatched roof allows the house to breathe. They make a fire inside the house to keep the mosquitoes away. In the new houses they did the same, and when they woke up in the morning they were covered with soot trapped inside the asbestos roof—which had the additional disadvantage of producing echoes. The Gongawas value secrecy, and do not like anyone to overhear their conversation. This fear is perhaps rooted in traditional religion. The new houses had the effect of introducing a devil or another god who created echoes in their dwellings. So they went back to their banco (rammed earth) buildings.

The architect's spaces were dictated by economy instead of what the Gongawa would have defined as a compound. Each family was alloted only three houses, so that families and

Fig. 31. Traditional houses in a Gongawa village in Nigeria

Fig. 32. Architect's attempted improvement of traditional Gongawa houses

livestock, chickens, and goats were all mixed up, resulting in a lot of social mess.

Tema, Ghana

Tema, a new suburb of Accra, was contemporary to the Gongawa resettlements in the sense that it grew out of the industrial infrastructure that the Ghana government embarked upon several years ago. It was a bigger dream and a bigger vision. The new city of Tema was programed to tie in with the industrial base that was to be generated by the Volta Dam project. The city has grown all by itself because it has all the elements to make it grow. But, again, the problem of planning comes in because the traditions of mixed activities—housing, living, selling in one area—were not sufficiently considered.

The planned markets, segregated from other uses, are underused. (Fig. 33) In the settlement itself the people started building kiosks near their homes. They converted their garages and verandas into shops. In other words, they reasserted the pattern of life they were accustomed to, with living and selling mixed together. (Fig. 34)

The separation of residential areas from business areas, borrowed from Western European and American planning, does not work. It might work in 50 years, when everybody has perhaps reached that point in his search for identity. Again, selling activity in West Africa is not really determined on the basis of cost and profit. For a great many people it is a social activity.

Technological Possibilities of Banco

I like to use the word "banco" instead of mud, because the English word "mud" does not adequately describe this material. "Banco" is a French word adapted from the Bambera language to describe this building material. Banco is able to do almost anything you could ask it to do. In Niger and parts of Nigeria people have been able to use banco to build very thin shell structures without reinforcement that measure about 12 feet in

Fig. 33. Underused market in Tema, Ghana

Fig. 34. Commercial structures appear in residential areas

diameter and about 12 feet high. Comparing banco shells to
reinforced concrete, this is a tremendous achievement. Instead
of trying to substitute new materials, we should ask the
scientists and engineers to improve traditional materials.

I cannot presume to speak for all the developing countries,
but in Nigeria we need specific proposals or projects that
highlight the problems of cities and villages in terms of making
transitions from what they are to what they would like to be.
If one thinks of Lagos or Ibadan, for instance, the people of
each are peculiar to themselves. Even though Lagos shares
many problems with New York City or London, the fact
remains that the way people in Lagos use spaces is peculiar to
Lagos, and therefore the problems must be highlighted on that
basis.

When one goes from Lagos into the countryside, he sees
that what is needed is not brand-new settlements or very
sophisticated equipment, but practical ways in which to solve
problems like those of water supply, drinking water, and
movement.

Therefore, to make any meaningful contribution to the
life of such people as the Dogon, we must localize each problem
and think of solutions in terms of the place. Each society is
unique in terms of the sociology of the people and their living
habits. If more attention is paid to these factors then in the
long run every settlement will be appropriately individualized.

Appropriate Building Systems

APRODICIO LAQUIAN

The bias in the Western rich nations is toward the individual. The bias in the poor countries is familial, communal, or even national, rarely individual. While the poor may worry about what is the heat loss or gain of an individual, they also worry about the heat loss or gain of three or four persons sharing the same mat under the same mosquito net, living together very closely.

Human settlement systems include hard dynamic systems and social systems that are just as real. Is it because social systems are social that we tend to push them into the background? There is a bias toward physical systems—winds, radiation, heat loss—and against the less predictable, less quantifiable and less knowable social systems.

The Philippines imported a housing factory from the Federal Republic of Germany. The factory can put a dwelling unit together in three hours. The unit costs about four times the average income of persons in the squatter areas. The labor input from the squatters is practically nil, and their repayment capacity for the cost of the house not much more—yet this was the hard system that "expert advisors" suggested. Specific innovations as such are less important than the following parts of the settlement system:

The policy framework within which innovation should take place. This means the policymakers, their attitudes and values, their biases and prejudices.

The administrative system: The capability of managers to bring about the specific changes. Not just at the pilot stage, which is quite easy if you can get somebody inspired, but at a large enough scale to bring it down to the level of the specific squatter or slum-dweller.

The resource capability: How much can the people pay for this innovation? How long will it take them to evolve and pay for these kinds of improvements? Where do you put all these innovations?

The spatial systems: Should development be concentrated in cities that are already drowning in their own sewage and piling people on top of each other, or should you try to decentralize? What are the costs and benefits of decentralization? What kind of economies of scale can you produce?

There is the Utopian empirical bias from which most of us look at innovations. Given Utopian circumstances, you can come up with innovations. One of the most important biases we have right now is the confidence that once a problem is diagnosed, once we decide we are going to the moon, once we decide we need a shelter like an Eskimo igloo, then research and development can deliver the innovations.

Well then, how about looking at it the other way around? I am particularly interested in housing and the building industry—a sector that generally makes use of what there is rather than creating new forms. Houses are built from whatever is available—rusty galvanized iron sheets, cement, steel—

whatnot. Local builders rarely invest in research and
development. In taking what is available, the community is a
resource. Slums and squatter areas not only provide cheap labor
for housing, but many other resources. (Figs. 35, 36, 37)

We should erase the bias of finite evolution: the biases of
innovators and technicians that think in terms of a finite house,
a finite city, a finite system of settlements.

A dynamic evolutionary concept is needed, in which we
do not start with the buildings already arranged in a specific
manner, but with structures that can have dynamic evolutionary,
change-oriented focuses.

The World Bank, evaluating a transport system for the
metro Manila area, advocated subways and monorails. The local
people said, "We have an incipient drop in the building
industry. Can we just import the engines from Japan. We can
make the chassis here and have a fleet of buses." The gap
between the subway-monorail people and the tinkerers, those
who want to make a jeepney out of a jeep, is so vast that they
are still discussing which is the right approach. (Fig. 38) This
kind of polarization serves to stress the nature of the debate.
The message up to now has been a high-technology message:
subways, monorails, tall vertical factories—and very little
attempt has been made to put them into the indigenous cultural
context.

The International Development Research Centre in
Canada is funding studies on specific techniques of evaluating
local level targets and local level indicators in cooperation with
the United Nations Research Institute on Social Development
in Geneva. Even though no physical changes are involved, this
is a technology, since it has an impact on settlements. Similarily,
the center is doing a study on service schemes, which include
rural services as part of the curriculum of professional schools.
The graduates, whether they be medical doctors or social
workers or engineers, are required by the government to bring
their skills back to serve their villages and find out what life
really is. This period of service is an integral part of their

Fig. 35. Self-built housing is usually constructed with ingenious use of whatever materials are available. In Salvador, Brazil, the city dump provides material

Fig. 36. Self-built housing in the Tondo Foreshore area, Manila, the Philippines

Fig. 37. With simple tools, Andean Indian villagers build a communal workshop. (Photo by International Labour Office)

Fig. 38. Such innovations as "jeepneys," like these in Manila, may provide appropriate intermediate technologies with immediate benefits

qualification for their professional degrees; it will affect their own performance, and in turn affect the community.

These soft technologies, or community technologies, respond to real world needs.

Using Intermediate Technologies

E. F. SCHUMACHER

First of all, what is intermediate technology? In developing countries a low-level technology exists that may fit in the main cities, but does not fit the large and heavily populated rural areas. The idea of intermediate technology is something very much better than the indigenous and often decayed technology in the rural areas, and at the same time infinitely more direct, less capital-intensive, less sophisticated than the rich man's technology.

It is always an extremely challenging moment when one has been talking about something for a long time and the question arises: am I just a talker or am I a doer? In order to start really doing, I set up a private company, with nonprofit status, called the Intermediate Technology Development Group (ITDG). The first thing ITDG did was to make a catalog, called *Tools for Progress*, of procurable small-scale equipment that might be useful for small-scale development in rural areas. (Fig. 39)

ITDG chose building as its first subject, on the very simple assumption that there can't be any development without some building going on—not just house building, but road building, or bridge building—any kind of building. Why is it that in most

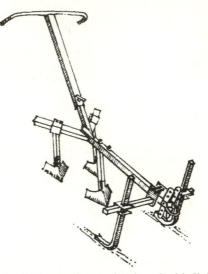

Fig. 39. An example of intermediate technology is this lightweight, multipurpose, animal-drawn implement, which can be used for plowing, ridging, hoeing, weeding, planting, carting, and other purposes

so-called developing countries, the slightly bigger building projects are immediately given to Western-type contractors? Why can't the developing countries do it themselves? Now as an economist, I know that it is really hard to accumulate capital in order to buy a building. If you don't do it yourself you are, in a manner of speaking, broke before you start. Why don't developing economies build what they need? At first we of ITDG thought this was perhaps mainly a technological question but it wasn't clear. A panel of experts from governments and from the professionals in building research was set up.

The panel advised that the bottleneck was not what had been thought. The technology of using local materials for local needs is quite different. It is the local contractors who have to hold it all together. The contractor can handle a contract for £500, but if it's for £600 he goes broke. While the professional institutions develop architects, quantity surveyors, and civil engineers, and the training institutes turn out plumbers and bricklayers; the contractors are the forgotten men. Training programs are necessary. In Nigeria, ITDG developed an extensive training program for the small local contractor, which was a great success. A large amount of tested training material and visual aids were produced.

The next need was water because there can't be any development without it, and many of the developing countries are in very arid zones. Analogous to the building panel, a panel of experts on water was set up. It developed small-scale technology for water storage, water improvement, and water purification. Underground rainwater catchment tanks that ITDG first tried out in Botswana have since been applied in many parts of the world. After that a panel on small-scale power was established, and then perhaps the most important, one on agricultural equipment. Instead of going through all the specialized panels, of which there are now fifteen, I would like to make one general point.

Our group is called Intermediate Technology Development Group *Limited*, and we are indeed extremely limited. But there are many other people who do similar work. One of the tragedies is that there are no communications channels between groups. Things are left very often to accidental meetings. An international communication system at this level of self-help technology is needed so that people in this area can learn from one another's successes and also from one another's mistakes. Meanwhile, ITDG has been instrumental in setting up groups similar to ours in quite a number of countries. These groups don't belong to ITDG in any sense, but they have been inspired by it. Sometimes they are situated within the university. For instance in the University of Kumasi, Ghana, based on its work there is a very active group that is supported from the USA; in India there are governmental and private groups; and several more in Latin America.

In order to facilitate communication, ITDG has launched an international journal called *Appropriate Technology Quarterly*. It counteracts the present situation in which, at the rich man's level of technology, there is an absolutely first-class commu-

nication system, but on the poor man's level of technology,
there is none. This is immensely frustrating. The scientists
and technologists of the rich countries work on the problems
of the rich countries and the scientists and technologists (far
less numerous) of the poor countries also work on the problems
of the rich countries.

Technology as a Political Factor

It is a false distinction to say "technology won't settle it, it's a
political or an institutional problem." Each particular type of
technology is itself a political and social shaping agent, with
far-reaching sociological implications.

Technology grows bigger and bigger and more and more
complex, always requiring bigger starting capital, and therefore
being reserved for people already rich and powerful. If resources
are not engaged to create a technology, or, if it already exists, to
assemble and systematize one that is accessible to the small
people in the rural areas and the urban slums; if this dependency
is not counteracted, then no amount of change at the political or
social, or any other level, will help, because the people cannot
help themselves, and will remain as dependent on the rich and
powerful as they were before.

All I am asking is not to extend the perfectly legitimate
political and sociological argument in a way that invalidates the
technological approach. Both are necessary. A political change,
unless supported by an appropriate technology, will be just a
paper change, will be just another gang of people trying to do
different things because they haven't got the appropriate
technology.

For example, an African government was most anxious to
deal with malnutrition, which is a protein deficiency, by
fostering egg production. But when I visited the egg producers,
I found them all in despair, with eggs lying on the floor,
because they couldn't get packaging material to send the eggs
to market.

On getting back to London, I found that all the egg trays
in the world are made by one multinational company. They

might be persuaded to build a factory at Lusaka, if the market warranted it. How many egg trays were needed? The smallest manufacturing unit (costing a quarter million British pounds) produces a million trays a month. That was the number Zambia required in a year, at least to start with. Short of organizing an all-African common market for egg trays, there was nothing to be done with the multinational corporation.

I said to myself, "It cannot be beyond the wit of man to make egg trays." In Africa there is plenty of fiber—some is even exported. ITDG engaged various resources to produce a miniplant which, with one-fortieth of the capacity of the multinational corporation, produces egg cartons at one-fortieth of its price.

The political and sociological consequences of the existence of this miniplant are very profound. It's no use talking about self-sustaining or relatively self-sustaining communities unless there is a miniplant technology. It's no use talking about decentralized modes of living without small-scale technology. There is no contradiction between saying "an appropriate technology must be created" and saying "the basic problems are political and sociological" because there's an inherent relationship between the two.

Low-Cost Housing Technology: Problems, Issues, and a Proposed Solution

LOUIS J. GOODMAN, ALBERT G. H. DIETZ, HASAN POERBO and *FREDRICH BURIAN*

L ow-cost housing represents a serious national problem in both developing and developed countries. While there are many ongoing efforts in low-cost housing, there is little interchange of problems and solutions. Multinational cooperative research and development programs can both provide a mechanism for communicating research results and a search for solutions to the multifaceted problems of providing minimal essential shelter.

The Technology and Development Institute (TDI) of the East-West Center, Hawaii, has stimulated the establishment of a network of cooperating institutions in Asia and the United States to undertake an action-oriented project concerning low-cost construction materials and design concepts for low-income family housing units in a variety of socioeconomic settings. This project includes research, professional development, and graduate degree study. The objective of this cooperative project is the provision of better housing for low-income family groups. The cost of housing to be studied is based on a general rule of thumb, adopted by a number of agencies concerned with this problem, which states that the cost should not exceed 2 to 2.5 times the annual income of a family for whom intended.

Problems and Issues

If the housing problem is to be solved in a practical way, it is important to formulate a program that will utilize as many local materials and skills as possible. It should leave for importation only that which is essential and will not interfere with primary economic development. Indeed, it should complement such development wherever possible. The problem cannot be solved by a quick recipe, but instead will require a multifaceted approach considering (1) planned utilization of land, (2) increased indigenous technical knowledge and skills, (3) increased use of indigenous building materials, (4) promotion of labor-intensive construction technologies, and (5) the development of suitable public policy and finance mechanisms. The solutions will require interdisciplinary interaction among architects, economists, engineers, and social scientists who will provide the necessary framework to view the totality of the numerous problems inherent in applying low-cost housing technology to different socioeconomic environments. Ultimately, the total spectrum of the problems of human settlements must be addressed, ranging from research and development on building materials and designs to methodology of physical planning, social and functional aspects of low-cost housing, and developing a viable indigenous building-industry base.

These goals can best be achieved by cooperative and coordinated research and development on a partnership basis involving both developing and developed societies. TDI is cultivating institutional relationships with US and Asian institutions, concerning the prospects of formulating mutual and cooperative research and development of low-cost construction materials and design concepts for low-income family housing units in a variety of socioeconomic settings.

Among the many problems and issues, the following form a system of influences and constraints that must be viewed as a whole.

Materials, Transportation and Production

1. To the fullest possible extent materials should be indigenous to avoid contributing to the depletion of often-scarce foreign exchange. However, where imported materials can clearly contribute to lowered costs and efficient use of indigenous materials, the imported materials should be considered.
2. Materials should be as light in weight as possible, to promote the transportation and erection of large shop-built components by simple processes.
3. Composites and assemblages should be utilized to the fullest possible extent, to make the most efficient use of materials and to obtain composite properties not attainable with the individual materials acting alone, and to reduce the number of components and parts that must be transported and assembled in the field. If, for example, roof and ceiling can be combined into one composite, the amount of material can often be reduced.
4. A two-pronged approach to the production of housing should be based on shop fabrication of simple and easily assembled components and on the application of labor-intensive, efficient field-assembly methods.

Sanitary Services

Analysis and treatment of water for domestic and industrial consumption and water-borne waste disposal should be considered as basic to housing. This should also be related to programs for garbage and refuse disposal, pest and insect control, food sanitation, and housekeeping.

Aggregating the Market

If any building system based on components produced in a shop for assembly at the site is to succeed, the demand must be reasonably predictable, since sporadic operations can cost more than conventional construction.

Labor

In many developing areas labor falls into two more or less distinct categories. The first consists of trained workers associated with established and growing industries. These people are quite secure in their jobs and reasonably well paid. They tend to form a more or less exclusive group. The second, usually larger category, comprises the unskilled or low-skilled underemployed workers, including casual laborers with no secure employment, doing whatever they can and receiving uncertain income. Often they badly need housing, but do not have the skills or organization to provide it by conventional building processes. On the other hand, their potential need is extremely large, if the means to utilize their abilities can be organized. A case study of a successful housing subdivision in the Philippines demonstrates how such labor can be organized and encouraged to provide its own housing on a partial self-help basis.[1]

Customs, Preferences and Prejudices

Every person spends his life in a home, has become attached and habituated to it, and is not easily diverted from the way of life associated with it. This results in a strongly conservative view respecting what constitutes a home. Custom, preference, and prejudice constitute strong, but not necessarily insurmountable, constraints to housing innovation.

Perhaps no other aspect of housing design is so difficult and important as this one. Research is badly needed to determine what constitutes socially acceptable housing. This entails searching for answers and guidance in explorations that are presently underway and it demands that new experiments be undertaken if these answers are not forthcoming.

Climate and Geography

If the cost of housing is to be kept as low as possible, undue reliance cannot be placed on mechanical means of controlling

living conditions. Housing must be designed to consider
carefully the climate and the weather, taking advantage of those
features that promote comfort, and minimizing those that do
not. The sun, prevailing winds, temperature and humidity
variations, and natural shading or favorable exposure must all
be considered so that the housing design can utilize them to
advantage or, where appropriate, minimize their effects.
Similarly, geographical features such as terrain, soil, ground
cover, earthquakes, and possibility of flooding must be
considered more critically than ever, because of increasing
densities and numbers of people.

Public Policy

Public policy can encourage or frustrate the development
of the level of housing production needed for combined
industrialization and rationalized field operation by action or
inaction with respect to financing, interest rates, building codes,
zoning laws, and provision of utilities and services. Most
important, if the political agencies, both nationally and locally,
support a steady policy, housing can proceed on an efficient
cost-reducing basis. If not, production becomes erratic and
costs rise. Many national, regional, and local housing authorities
have been set up with variable success. These, and housing
policies generally, need to be studied and the elements of
successful ones analyzed for possible adoption.

Information Acquisition and Dissemination

The need for effective methods of information acquisition,
processing, and dissemination is manifest in any organized
research and development effort. To a large measure, the
internal success of a research and development organization.
rests with its ability to scan appropriate information environments, have access to information relevant to its developmental
objectives, and identify gaps in information preliminary to the
conduct of original research. To just as great an extent, the
external success of an R and D organization depends upon its
ability to extend meaningfully the fruits of its efforts to

appropriate audiences and to receive feedback from those audiences.

In the complex and large-scale field of housing several recently-developed communication strategies (such as microforms and video tapes) may be employed to enhance information exchange among counterparts located at the far-flung corners of the world.

Project Management

There is need to improve the capabilities and skills of managers of a variety of public works projects, including housing. Indeed, this is such a vital issue in many countries that the East-West Technology and Development Institute (TDI) is presently formulating plans for a new activity concerned with development project management. The primary objective will be to develop in a number of countries a cadre of effective indigenous project managers with the necessary skills to successfully implement a project.

Cooperative International Network for Housing

TDI's cooperative action-oriented program is concerned with adapting, innovating, and diffusing low-cost construction material and design concepts for low-income family housing units. The major objective is to enhance the capabilities of participating institutions to make their own research more effective through collaborative study and exchange of information regarding common problems and solutions.

The vehicle to accomplish overall project objectives is the network of cooperating institutions in Asia and the United States. Research and development is primarily but not exclusively focused on the production aspect of housing as a formative process in the development of human settlements. Utilization of local materials and skills, innovative designs, and application of the most appropriate technologies are central problems in the project. In-country linkages with national housing authorities, developers, construction industries, and financial institutions are essential.

The project strategy encourages country participants to decide for themselves which area of research they wish to pursue within the general framework of the cooperative research plan. It can be anticipated that participating institutions will have their own strengths and weaknesses, and that conditions will be different from country to country. Cooperation among the institutions is interpreted here in terms of a continuous and systematic exchange of experience and information, and, whenever possible, also an exchange of personnel and mutual assistance, with the objective of supplementing and accelerating the knowledge of housing among the participants and, consequently, enhancing the comprehensiveness of the entire project. The TDI project team will continue cooperative research endeavors with the institutions in the embryonic network to provide the necessary catalytic input regarding new ideas on low-cost housing, as well as to implement plans for the recommended information-exchange network. Details of three activities for fiscal year 1974–1975 are given below, as examples.

Research

The role of TDI involves a continuing review, evaluation, and dissemination of available information about low-cost construction materials and innovative design concepts by each of the cooperating institutions, concentrating on selection of building materials, structural design considering natural hazards, efficient and economical construction methods, functional roofing systems, and sanitary considerations. In addition, reviews of the role of national housing authorities and other in-country linkages, such as construction industries, create an awareness and understanding of the functions and activities of each group concerned with housing.

Roving Workshop

Roving workshops primarily intend to make on-the-spot observations of actual research and development activities underway at each of the five institutions, and to examine the capability and potential of each.

The first roving workshop, convened in January 1975, was made up of a core group of two representatives each from the five institutions involved in the cooperative network, along with three TDI members. At the five-day visits in Indonesia, the Philippines, and Hawaii, the core group was augmented by an additional thirty to forty persons coming from a representative cross-section of university, government, and private sectors with a demonstrated interest in, and power to provide housing for low-income families. A second roving workshop in October 1975 pursued a similar sequence in Thailand, Korea, and Hawaii.

Documentation

Systematic visual documentation is employed to record research conducted at network institutions. Audio and visual information collected periodically by appropriate network personnel, together with comprehensive documentation during the roving workshops, is used to track project development.

One significant result anticipated is that each cooperating institution will be able to draw upon the experience of the others through on-the-spot observations of ongoing research and development and through systematic information-dissemination linkages. Another result should be the development of active in-country linkages with relevant groups such as national housing authorities and construction industries. A third significant result should be to start pulling together the necessary forces from public and private sectors and from financial institutions to implement the new methods of producing low-cost housing.

The East-West Center's Role

The East-West Technology and Development Institute's role is that of catalyst and coordinator. It will (1) convene miniconferences and roving workshops to provide forums for

exchange of results, problems, and ideas, (2) provide new
research ideas on low-cost construction materials and design
concepts, and low-cost water-supply and waste-disposal
systems, (3) organize a strategy for developing in-country
linkages with various groups from public and private sectors
concerned with the housing problem, (4) initiate evaluation of
research and development activities at network institutions, and
(5) implement plans for information exchange within the
network and with other organizations involved with similar
activities in different parts of the world.

In this role, the TDI, in concert with representatives of the
cooperating institutions, plans and organizes periodic meetings,
during which common problems and solutions are explored, the
degree of necessary overlapping effort ascertained, the areas
requiring further examination determined, and the kinds of
action needed to implement research and development planned.
These meetings are held on a rotating basis at the cooperating
institutions to provide the participants with firsthand familiarity
with each other's activities, as well as with the problems in their
respective regions. The actual research and development is performed by each institution. Furthermore, the process of integration of policy research and action-oriented R and D into actual
housing and construction is deliberately left open to the various
parties concerned since conditions vary from country to country.

Programs at Cooperating Research and Development Institutes

In the Asian countries initially involved in this program, the
research and development institutes are in a position to play a
key role in the implementation of cooperative programs. They
are relatively unique in these areas in having the capability of
doing the necessary research, carrying it through the
development stage, and bringing it to the attention of public and
private agencies in a position for implementation. To carry out
these functions successfully, the research institutes need to
stretch their own scarce resources, which are limited by

legislation primarily to technology and design. They need to draw on the resources of other agencies working on the broad aspects of public policy, the social aspects of housing, labor, population, economics, and finance. Furthermore, the research institutes need to reach out beyond their own particular regions to explore common efforts being carried on in other regional institutes, and to explore common requirements bearing on housing in those regions. Beyond this, however, they need to be cognizant of similar problems in other parts of the world, such as Latin America and Africa, where solutions that are applicable to the Asian areas may have been sought and found. They also need to draw upon the experience of areas where industrialization and housing technology are considerably advanced, such as Europe, North America, and Japan, in order to determine not only to what extent the technology is applicable, but what the social, political, and economic constraints have been, how the market has been aggregated, and how the whole process has been organized and managed.

The individual research institutes, although they occupy potentially key positions in housing in their respective countries, tend to operate in isolation from each other and from the activities of the rest of the world. They lack good mechanisms to bring about closer liaison among themselves, and to obtain access to developments elsewhere. They are, therefore, less effective than they could be in this critical area.

It is the aim of this program to encourage the development of such links among the research institutes and to extend these links to other institutes through collaborative action-oriented research and development and the development of a common information system. It is planned to include the University of Hawaii through its departments of Civil Engineering, Architecture, and Sociology in this embryonic network. The research institutes are strategically situated, and their number is not too large to preclude effective coordination. As the program progresses and its operations are refined, other institutions can be added to this network.

Examples of Low-Cost Housing Research and Development

There are a number of examples of research and development efforts resulting in low-cost housing units for low-income families in both Asia and the United States.[2] A project team at the Asian Institute of Technology (AIT) in Bangkok, Thailand, is investigating the use of locally-produced asbestos-cement sheets for both exterior walls and roofing systems. The results of this team effort are illustrated in Figures 40 and 41. The cost does not include land, which is on the AIT campus. The cost of labor is approximately 20 percent of the total.

A research team at the University of the Phillippines, including members from the Colleges of Engineering and Architecture and the Institute of Planning, is conducting research on "development of design criteria and methodology for the low-cost, low-rise buildings to better resist external winds." Figure 42 shows one of two experimental low-cost houses designed and constructed as a part of this research study. In this case, as in the AIT prototype, the cost does not include land.

Fig. 40. One of two prototype duplex houses built on the campus of the Asian Institute of Technology, Bangkok, Thailand. Each unit has approximately 50 square meters of floor area, and cost in early 1974 US$1,250 per unit, or $25 per square meter

Fig. 41. Wall and roof detail for Asian Institute of Technology prototype house. The longitudinal walls are supported by lightly reinforced concrete grade-beams poured monolithically with floor slabs. The rigidity of corrugated asbestos-cement eliminates need for columns in the walls, and purlins and rafters in the roof. The latter is supported on 2-by-6-inch timber headers bolted to the top of the longitudinal wall.

Fig. 42. The disks on the roof and walls of this experimental house at the Science Garden, University of the Philippines, are sensors to monitor the wind pressure on the house, to test its resistance. The double walls and ceilings are made of locally produced modularized chipboard panels, and the roof, of galvanized iron sheets. The direct construction costs of this 46-square-meter house in 1973 were US$1,000.

A low-cost housing unit in Korea is shown in Figure 43. The exterior walls are constructed of stabilized soil building blocks, and the roofing system consists of asbestos-cement tiles.

Indonesia has long been active in the area of low-cost housing development. A prototype low-cost house built in the early 1970s is illustrated in Figure 44.

In one of the highest cost-of-living areas in the United States, the island of Oahu in the state of Hawaii, the Hawaii Community Design Center, staffed by three VISTA architects, has designed and built a prototype "Minimum House" intended for self-help construction. A photograph of the completed house and a representative page from a step-by-step self-help building manual are shown in Figures 45 and 46. The construction cost in 1974 was $5,500 including all materials, but excluding the cost of labor and land. This is indeed a remarkable feat in an area where low-cost housing generally falls in the $25,000 to $35,000 range.

An outstanding illustration of a pilot project adapting local soil and cement as low-cost building materials is found at Mindanao State University, Marawi City, Philippines. A Cinva-

Fig. 43. This prototype house was built by the Bureau of Housing and Urban Planning, Ministry of Construction, South Korean Republic. It has a total floor area of 40 square meters; the cost of construction was US$747 in 1970/1971, reducible to $600 with self-help labor, and to less than $500 with self-production of blocks

Fig. 44. A prototype housing unit in a project for low- and middle-income families. Designed and built by the Regional Housing Center, Bandung, Indonesia, the house has 45 square meters of floor area, walls of woven bamboo mats, roof tiles of burned clay, and a total construction cost in 1970 of US$550, excluding land.

Fig. 45. The Hawaii Community Design Center "Minimum House," which has an area of 71 square meters, and is constructed of wood; the roof is made of asphalt sheets over plywood. The house is located on the grounds of the Waimanalo Community Center; several neighborhood families helped build it.

CUTTING GUIDE FOR PLYWOOD

USE A 2×4 AS A
CUTTING GUIDE FOR
THE SAW. CLAMP IT TO
THE PLYWOOD & RUN SAW
ALONG THE EDGE
OF IT.

C-CLAMP
2×4 OR 1×4 (MAKE SURE IT HAS A STRAIGHT EDGE)
DISTANCE FROM SAWBLADE TO EDGE OF GUARD
CUTTING LINE

PLYWOOD

POWER
CIRCULAR
SAW

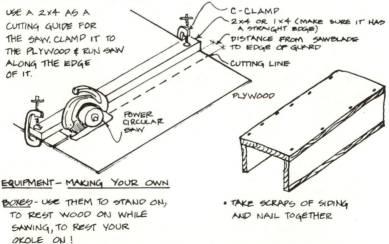

EQUIPMENT — MAKING YOUR OWN

BOXES - USE THEM TO STAND ON,
TO REST WOOD ON WHILE
SAWING, TO REST YOUR
OKOLE ON!

• TAKE SCRAPS OF SIDING
AND NAIL TOGETHER

Fig. 46. A draft page of the booklet being designed so that structures like the "Minimum House" can be built by self-help labor.

Fig. 47. The house utilizing soil-cement building blocks and floor tiles, constructed at Mindanao State University, the Philippines. The galvanized iron sheeting roof is nonfunctional; research continues to develop functional and lower cost roofing systems.

ram was used to produce the soil-cement building blocks and floor tiles. The total cost of the house shown in Figure 47 was US$600 (excluding land) in 1969–1970, for a floor area of 45 square meters. Labor accounts for approximately 30 percent of this total cost. Research is continuing, investigating soil-cement hollow blocks, soil-cement roofing panel systems and bamboo reinforcement.

REFERENCES

1. "A Housing Cooperative for Industrial Workers in Iligan City," in *Leadership Strategy in Development Projects: Public Leadership Workshop II, Part II, October 15–26, 1973* (Honolulu: East-West Center Technology and Development Institute).

2. *Cooperative Action-Oriented Research and Development in Low-Cost Housing Materials, Design and Construction: Supplemental Report Series No. 1*, August 1974 (Honolulu: East-West Center Technology and Development Institute).

Innovative Building Technology in Developed and Developing Countries

GERARD BLACHÈRE

I t is now widely recognized that the quality of housing is measured by how well it meets human requirements. Some of these requirements are absolute, like purity of air, hygiene, and safety, and some are related to the particular social, cultural, and economic environment, like space, rooms distribution, equipment, comfort, durability. A working group of the CIB (Conseil International du Batiment) has done a survey on human requirements. CIB is always working in this field and discussing method for improving the list of requirements—how they can be used by governments, designers, code writers, and others, and how they can be improved, what sort of research is needed, and so forth.

Quality and quantity are related by a very simple formula. We can devote the plus yielded by an improvement of productivity either to improving quality or to expanding quantity.

There are some specific obstacles to raising quantity: scarcity of skilled labor, energy, materials, and tools. The answer to raising quantity and bridging the gap of labor and energy and materials, is innovation. Innovation is also based on science. To try to innovate without a scientific base is a waste of time. To use science and technology even in their present state depends on adequate training for the architect and engineer.

The same technologies can be used in both developed and developing countries, but at different levels of sophistication— very simple in some cases and very sophisticated in others.

France now has a large factory producing large-panel technology. Vans are required to transport the panels to the site, and cranes to lift them into place. There is a much simpler way of fabricating panels—either of poured concrete, or of hollow blocks, without any skilled labor. Furthermore, on-site workshops can be used to eliminate the cost of transportation and the hazard of breakage en route.

It is often said that panel technology leads to poor architecture. But poor architecture results from a lack of imagination. Imagination has been exercised to give at least variety, if not great architecture to large panel buildings which have curved walls, "traditional" style façades, or almost any other style.

There is also a technology using concrete parts in what we call "Meccanos," after the children's building toy. A lot of schools have been built out of standard concrete parts ordered from a catalog. This system is very popular in France for low-rise housing.

Three-dimensional concrete modules are heavyweight modules, but have the advantage that they can be completed in the plant, so that three-dimensional volumes, sometimes even furnished, are delivered at the site.

Other building technologies are based on lightweight sandwich systems of expanded polystyrene cores between sheets of asbestos cement, Meccanos with steel-framed floors that incorporate conduits for electrical and heat installations, and three-dimensional modules with steel frames and lightweight panels.

Most of these technologies that have been used in Europe have the potential of a parallel development, utilizing local materials and very low investment.

Innovative Building Technologies: Productivity

HERMANN RUHLE

The building industry all over the world is faced with problems—especially the problems of cost—this industry swallows huge amounts of money. Research workers, design engineers, and contractors worldwide consider the production of low-cost building a very real, serious problem. During the last ten years building costs have shown a steady upward trend, the main cause being the considerable increase of wages in many countries.

The major factors influencing building costs vary: high wages with a steady upward trend in industrialized countries, and deficiencies in building materials like steel, plastics, and others in developing countries. In countries like the German Democratic Republic, Czechoslovakia, and Poland, where new industries are developing, such steel as is available is allocated to manufacturing industries in preference to construction.

Some countries use construction materials such as bricks or poured on-site concrete; their use, based on manual craftsmanship and building practices, has proven extremely economical. In discussing general trends in the construction industry, we must consider not only technical advantages, new techniques, and modern architectural concepts, but also the complex economic and political aspects that differ from country to country.

As far as low-cost building is concerned, only the most effective and inexpensive techniques will prevail. The most important criterion for choosing this type of structure is the cost breakdown. Some of the building techniques are panel, slab-and-beam, and box. Infill elements like panels, windows, doors, partitions, flooring, air-conditioning, painting, insulation, and water supply represent approximately 60 to 75 percent of the total cost. The upward trend continues.

In countries with sharply rising wages, but comparatively stable materials costs, the effort should be to equalize the difference between the cost of building and the cost of production of industrial goods. At present, site labor represents approximately half the total cost of conventional building. In recent years the use of prefabricated steel and concrete modular elements has reduced the need for on-site labor. This speaks in favor of large-series production in the building industry. However, special plants for producing building units require high capital investment. The alternative, standardization and modular construction, has met a great deal of opposition in many countries for ideological and philosophical reasons.

In countries where wages are low, the construction industry uses, in the main, manual craftsmanship and traditional techniques, which are often most economical, not only for individual houses and community buildings, but also for large-span industrial construction.

Today and in the future the enormous need for buildings all over the world can be met by planning large-series production; but standardization and modular construction must form an integral part to guarantee its success.

It is important to inventory building materials and the environmental factors that affect human settlements for every country. Since the problems of fire-resistance of materials, insulation, stress, problems of color and design, are different in different countries, the answers can be successful only when research has been thorough, both on existing conditions and on the specific suitability of the recommended solution.

Innovative Building Technologies: The Dome

R. BUCKMINSTER FULLER

You should approach any design problem by asking what the task is that you want to accomplish. You certainly don't design an aeroplane or a radio in order to recycle some waste material. That's not how you get there at all. You consider what is required, how it is to function, and how to solve the problem in the most economical way possible. If this requires using an ounce of titanium or some other valuable element, you can afford it, because you will have deduced that any substitute would be more costly.

The building industry has been strictly a common-sense industry, and couldn't be more remote from science in approaching the problems of housing mankind. I believe in dealing with these problems from a scientific, rational point of view. In producing shelter, what I call design science must take full responsibility from the beginning all the way through. What are the needs and limits of human beings—what do they *really* need, and then how do you get them what they want? You must be responsible not just for designing the building, but for how it is produced. You must know exactly what it costs, where the material will come from, how it is built, how it is serviced, and how, ultimately, it is disposed of and the materials recycled. In the meantime, you get high performance out of it, and study how to get more performance with the same amount of material.

Domes enclose the greatest volume with the least surface, so that you get the most economical undertaking that way. Flat sheets have no structural strength. Compound curvatures, which can be composed of triangles, bear by far the greatest load for the same amount of material. Thus, compound curvatures give you greater strength and spheres give you the most volume, which is why Nature didn't house heads, oranges, or eggs in cubes, but in spheroidal structures. This is what brought me to the Geodesic dome and other lightweight structures. Around the world, there are now over a hundred thousand Geodesic structures, which can enclose any given space and stand up against hurricanes and earthquakes. These domes have gone all over the world into places where nothing else would do the task.

On top of Mount Fuji there is a beautiful Geodesic weather station. It is the only thing that can take the enormous weather and fantastic winds, yet it is light enough to be lifted two and a quarter miles into the air by helicopter.

In December 1973 a great Geodesic dome was put right over the South Pole for an enterprise called Project Deep Freeze. The dome is made out of stainless steel and aluminium, strong enough to support snow loads of 300 pounds to the square foot, but light enough so that a couple of airplanes could deliver it, and simple enough, too, so that men would not perish before getting it up.

There is a whole new generation coming up that is free of of stereotypes. We have for instance, been making skis and surfboards out of polyester, fiberglass, and the like, and are really very expert. Now we have suddenly gone over to making Geodesics. The kids are finding that they can get themselves a home (when standard houses are costing US$20,000 to $30,000) for $300 to $400. A nice home—one that will take the snow loads and is cosy and has some mystical sense of being right, and goes along with the sense of truthfulness of the young.

Speaking of mass production, we now have many kinds of sheeting that can be used to cover this type of dome; over a hundred countries make some suitable type of material. We can get steel, corrugated Kraft paper, and plastics that are delivered on rolls. When you use paper (coated with plastic to make it weatherproof) you can print the geometric directions right on it, full scale, so that the recipient just has to fold on the dotted line, as if he were making up a paper box.

On the Lower East Side of New York City, I have been trying to help the gangs who are trying to develop their own economic support. Somehow they don't enjoy government support or charities. They are very independent. Most of these kids were high on drugs and had dropped out of school. It is amazing, but we were able to teach them spherical trigonometry in six months, and they put up their own dome. There is gang warfare there in that slum neighborhood, and a rival gang burnt the dome down. I showed the boys how they could re-cover the structure, and now they have a fireproof dome that will stand all the tests that rival gangs can give it.

There were to be Pan-American games held in Santo Domingo, and something to house an enormous number of people was needed. With the help of some big paper manufacturers, we found we could produce domes fast enough to take care of the problem. We were turning out literally thousands a day, at the rate of US$150 for a 20-foot dome. This is really quite ample for an average family. With a cement floor added, you could have a fireproof home for about US$300. So we now have the means of coping with emergencies, such as earthquakes.

Every time we have a great disaster, our domes are proposed as a solution for emergency shelter. But then it turns out that nothing is more of a political handout than a building contract. The building industry is powerful enough to say that this innovation won't be allowed to happen. So I decided in 1927 to start at the North Pole where there is no building industry to interfere, and esthetics were not an issue—to start under the most formidable physical conditions—and then let the dome work in towards society. The first practical application that really was a success was on the Distant Early Warning (DEW) line, where my domes ring the Arctic. They are in all the places where nothing else will do. So nobody can say they don't work, because, in fact, they are the only things that do. Now they are really being accepted, and I feel we are pretty well on target. I have now been at it 47 years, and I said it would take about 50 years. I have been delivering domes by helicopter for fifteen years, and now it's quite possible to deliver a dome to cover a whole football stadium. We could bring you a whole city in one day.

Innovative Building Technologies: Water-Free Waste Disposal

CARL LINDSTROM

The main reason for water pollution from households is that they use water as a transportation medium for soluble wastes from toilet and kitchen. In fact, each household uses about 55,000 gallons a year for this purpose. Consequently, the most logical and effective way to decrease this kind of pollution is to develop and use sanitation technologies that do not depend on water.

The present system for disposing of solid and liquid waste is not only destructive of natural ecological cycles, but is also unnecessary. If the organic materials, including soiled paper that is now disposed of as solids, were mixed with toilet wastes, the conditions for composting processes would be almost ideal. The balance between carbon, nitrogen, and phosphorus would be favorable, as would the heat production and moisture in the material. Such a mixture would have great importance for the end product and its value as a fertilizer. For, unlike chemical synthetic fertilizers, this end product would also contain trace metals like sodium, iron, magnesium, zinc, and so forth, which are critical to balance soil conditions. The structure of this combination of waste materials would be a humus soil, with an odor reminiscent of composted leaves. The average amount produced would correspond to a few buckets per person per year. Perhaps most significant, however, is the fact that the organic waste, including the toilet part, can be processed safely and hygienically within the dwelling into an end product that is not only harmless, but positively useful.

Considering the extent to which the burden on the soil is reduced when the toilet wastes are removed from the grey water (from bath, dishes, and laundry), leaving a relatively easy task for natural processes in the soil to deal with the remaining pollutants, the first step is to separate solid organic wastes (toilet and kitchen) from grey water.

The Clivus Compost-Reactor

The compost equipment is the main element in the system. The Clivus compost-reactor works on the physical principles of gravity, capillary action, and ventilation. (Fig. 48) The composting material is enclosed in an impervious container which is connected to the toilet and kitchen refuse openings by means of two chutes. A vent provides a means of escape for the gases produced by decomposition processes.

A layer of topsoil placed on the sloping bottom contains the bacteria necessary to the decomposition of the toilet and kitchen wastes. The feces which accumulate in the upper chamber also contain bacteria necessary to aerobic decomposition.

Urine is drained off down the sloping bottom to be decomposed by nitrobacteria existing in the soil, thus forming nitrates and carbon dioxide. This is the same process by which urine deposited on the soil in nature is decomposed. As the urine drains out of the excrement chamber, air is able to reach the breathing organisms that break down feces. As the material decomposes, carbon dioxide and water vapor leave the container through the vent and the volume decreases correspondingly.

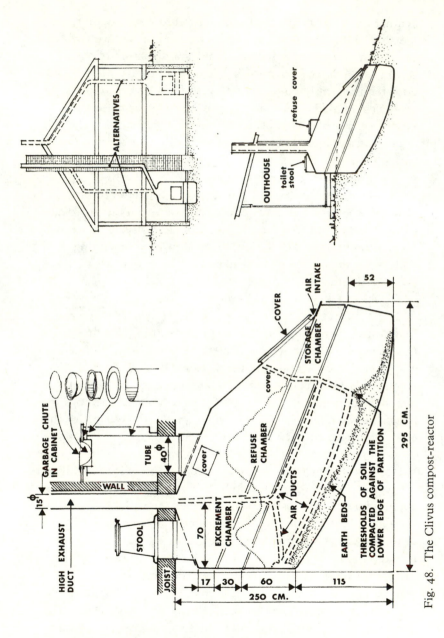

Fig. 48. The Clivus compost-reactor

As the kitchen refuse decomposes, the high proportion of cellulose present in this material produces heat, which helps to evaporate the liquids, thus further reducing the volume. The first stage of the process, in which the larger particles are broken down and the greatest heat is produced, is quite rapid. The secondary process—the mineralizing of the material—takes months or years.

The ventilation duct can either extend above the roof or vent into a chimney. Because the inside of the converter is kept at a lower pressure than the outside, there is no odor either in the bathroom or in the kitchen when the covers are opened.

The total amount of finished compost produced per person per year is about 10 gallons of soil. A conventional toilet uses and pollutes 10,000 gallons of clean water per person per year just to transport these wastes.

According to tests made at the National Swedish Bacteriological Laboratory on eight different samples, there are no findings of *E. coli* bacteria in the final product. This is most likely due to the inhospitable nature of the environment at the lower end where the composted soil slowly emerges. This material is almost completely mineralized and can support only the soil bacteria. These also consume most pathogens. The composter is practically fail-safe because:

1. There is no turning or stirring in the unit.

2. The turnover speed is very low. It takes approximately 2 to 3 years for the soil particles to run through the reactor.

3. The construction makes it almost impossible to take out material that is not mineralized.

A prototype was built in 1939—then World War II interfered, and consequently the idea was not developed until 1964, when the process was first described in a public paper. After that some new prototypes were built and studied for improvements. Typical early problems were the continuity of the process inhibiting said concentrations, ventilation, and of course general lack of various long-range experience.

The present design has been installed in about thirteen hundred Scandinavian homes. A multiapartment project is being carried out in Finland in a two-story, four-apartment building. The main concerns are capacity and end product.

Innovative Transport Technologies: The Vertebrate Train

ALEJANDRO GOICOECHEA OMAR

When transportation systems develop, they improve the social and economic life of isolated settlements, as well as the interchange of people and things between them. The technology of transport undoubtedly has an important influence on the development of settlements.

The availability of goods to people depends upon it. If this market relationship is not satisfactory, it creates an obstacle to social, political, and economic development. New settlements develop according to the availability of transport facilities. Settlements that grow up along the railway track, grow steadily in importance as long as transportation improves.

For large parts of the world, collective transportation by railroad is undoubtedly the mass transportation system for today. Trains cannot run by air or by road, but they have a monopoly on large capacity, unlike road transport. The only disadvantage of railroad transport is that it follows a fixed route. It is not free, it has to run at a certain speed, it has to stop, it has to follow certain routes. On the other hand, road transport is much slower when road capacity is saturated with vehicles.

Mass transport has been paralyzed by a lack of improved railroad technology. The life of the conventional train is over. It cannot solve the problem of deficit, nor the problem of safe circulation, nor the economic problem. There is undoubtedly a lot of railroad infrastructure in the world which cannot be eliminated, and there are interests which must be respected, but only if they do not obstruct progress.

We must consider the technical concepts of a transport system: (1) speed—transport without speed is not useful; (2) economy—a prohibitively expensive technology is likewise not useful; (3) safety—an unsafe technology is clearly unacceptable.

Conventional railways have fundamental problems of safety and efficiency, and are uneconomical as well. We need a new method of transportation that overcomes these problems, and can be usefully applied to human settlements. This concern is evident all over the world. England, the USA, Germany, France, and Japan are all researching new transportation methods that will be fast, safe, and economical. Japan, Germany, and France in particular have made great strides towards the creation of new unconventional methods. They have turned up some very interesting ideas that will be useful in the future—for instance, the magnetic system and the air-cushion system.

One of the technical defects in the design of conventional trains is that each pair of wheels is fixed to an axle, which does not allow flexibility of movement. There is a moment, on curves, in which one of the wheels should turn faster than the other, but as they are fixed, they run at the same speed. This is a mechanical mistake. There is also a series of friction phenomena, well known to classical technicians, which they have been trying to improve by designing conical tires, but this does not entirely solve the problem, which is that the greater length of the outer rail in relation to the inner rail on curves produces derailment of the train at high speeds. This happens because the wheels and the axle are powerfully set into the track, and guided only by the flange of the wheel. This was the reason why, in the 1920s, I decided to make a radical change to the classical technology. I saw the necessity of creating a free wheel, not fixed to the axle.

Another problem of the conventional train is its weight, which is necessary to prevent derailment. The first thing I had to do to solve this problem was to find a procedure by which the wheels could not get off the tracks, without depending on greater weight to keep the car in place. Weight is an enemy of economy. The rail acts directly on the flange. If the rail does not touch the flange, its task is to support, not to guide. Using the classical design of the curve, the exterior wheel mounts the rail by means of the flange. But why does the wheel not mount the rail? Because of the weight. We are lost, because we are slaves of the weight, the structure must increase as well, and when the structure increases, building costs are higher. All this obstructs mechanical progress, and explains current railroad deficits.

Birth of the Talgo Train

When, in the conventional train, I reduced the weight to half, a new train was born in Spain, called "El Talgo." This train was received in the way all innovations are received—with a lot of skepticism. Nowadays, the Talgo is accepted as one of the best trains in the world. It took twenty years to convince the people and the government to accept the Talgo as a mass transport medium.

The Vertebrate Train

The vertebrate train is safer than conventional trains because the wheels are mounted at its center of gravity. The characteristics of the vertebrate train are like the ones of the Talgo, but they are more perfected. It is, let's say, an elevated Talgo. Why is it elevated? Simply to avoid derailments. There is a phenomenon that technicians cannot deny—the fact that the safety of the conventional train depends on the wheel flanges. The center of gravity is located at a height of 1.20 m, and when the train makes a turn there is a centrifugal force acting on this center of gravity so that the resistance goes to the flange. Then the train overturns. To counteract this tendency the level or the slope of the tracks must be changed. But in fact, what supports the train and keeps it from derailment is the pressure of the flange against the rail. This is the difficulty of conventional trains.

What we have to do in order to avoid derailment is to raise the rails to the same level as the center of gravity of the train; thus, the possibilities of overturning are zero, as are the chances of derailment. The train cannot derail as long as the track does not break. Another characteristic of the vertebrate train is light concentrated weight. How do we achieve this? By reducing the length of the cars from the standard 15 to 20 meters to 3 meters.

If an engine weighs 100 tons, the structure all along the line has to support these 100 tons, which means an expensive structure. In the case of the vertebrate train, the locomotive is eliminated, powering each individual car wheel independently (by electric motor). Thus, the 100 tons of engine are distributed all along the train, with correspondingly less weight to each wheel. All these advantages reduce the concentrated weight distribution. Conventional trains carry about six to ten tons per wheel; by contrast, the load is one ton in the vertebrate train. (Fig. 49)

As another consequence of the weight reduction we can utilize pneumatic wheels, making the ride smoother and quicker. Conventional trains do not have this alternative, and in addition, have the problems of operational deficits, being unsafe and lack economy—all of which are solved by the vertebrate trains. In sum, the vertebrate train is characterised by small concentrations of weight, total reversibility, no overturn, pneumatic wheels, and simplicity of construction.

The prototype vertebrate train was first built in 1969, in an unused Spanish train station. In this experimental line, 400 meters long, an above-ground structure was used. Y-shaped columns support pairs of parallel beams that, joined in sequence, provide supporting rails for the train. The beams are of prestressed concrete; their length varies according to the conditions where the train is to be installed, but normally they are produced in standard lengths of 10, 12, or 15 meters, so that they are not unwieldy and can be set up very fast on the site.

The coaches are fiberglass, cylindrical in section, accommodating 17 passengers each. Since they are only 3 meters

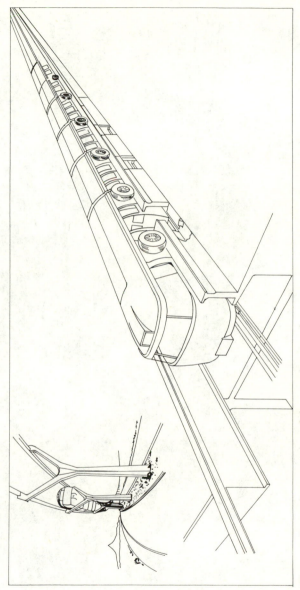

Fig. 49. General perspective of the vertebrate train

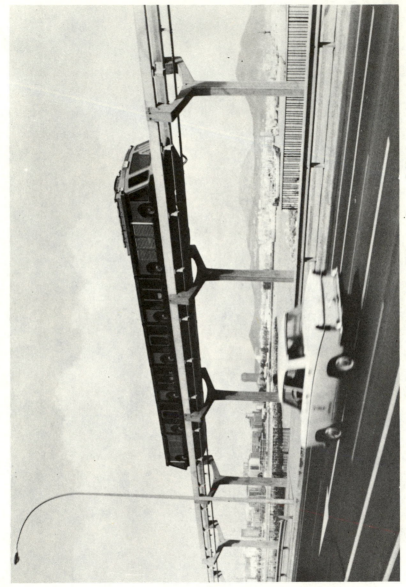

Fig. 50. Vertebrate train operating between airport and Las Palmas, Canary Islands

long, they are small enough to be transported in a large van. They are connected together by joints that are flexible in both horizontal and vertical directions, so that there is extreme flexibility in the whole train. Each coach has only two wheels, and is supported by the wheels and the joint to the next car, all placed at the center of gravity. The coach is thus supported in an entirely stable position, and cannot overturn or derail, while forming part of an extremely flexible whole.

One of the major innovations was to take the wheels from beneath the car, and place them midway up the side of the car, riding on rubber tires, along the beams. When the train arrives in the station, these beams must be opened up so as to free the door and let passengers get in or out. Therefore the beams alongside the loading platform are hinged, so that the appropriate sections will open up, like a drawbridge, when the train stops and the doors open.

An elevated demonstration track has been installed in the Canary Islands. It will be extended for 60 km to join the airport with the capital, Las Palmas. (Fig. 50) A line has also been designed for the city of Caracas, Venezuela. The train fits very well within the very complex urban structure of that densely populated city. Use has been made in this case of the riverbeds and ravines, and any other extra space. The line can be readily adapted to such spaces, and at very low cost.

Innovative Transport Technologies: The Airship

THEODOR WUELLENKEMPER

The Federal Republic of Germany has witnessed a renascence in the field of airship construction in recent years. Our experience has shown that the airship is a safe, inexpensive, and nonpolluting conveyance. An airship containing helium, a nonflammable gas, is self-supporting and therefore cannot crash. It is nonpolluting because the engines need only a small amount of thrust; it is economical because of the low cost of construction and maintenance. An airship can be built in a short period of time and is very simple to operate.

The Advantages of Freight Transportation by Airship

The airship can operate in areas and countries where roads, railways, and airplanes are inadequate or cannot exist. The main advantages of the airship are high capacity, low cost of production, and safety. Thus it meets all the requirements for use in the least developed and in developing countries. The airship can be built and assembled on the spot, and is therefore a very real alternative to conventional modes of transportation. Gondolas or containers are attached to the airship as passenger or freight containers. (Fig. 51)

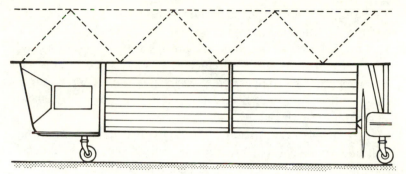

Gondola system utilized for containers

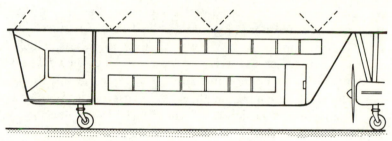

Passenger Gondola

Fig. 51. Interchangeable passenger (below) and freight (above) gondolas for airships

Technical Specifications

One cubic meter of helium carries one kilogram. One airship under construction at our plant contains 6,500 cubic meters of helium and can therefore carry 6.5 metric tons. The deadweight amounts to 3.5 tons, leaving a payload of 3 metric tons. Another airship contains 14,000 cubic meters of helium, with a carrying capacity of 10 tons and a length of 80 meters. Our new prototype, which we plan to complete in 1976, has a capacity of 80,000 cubic meters and a length of 120 meters, and will carry 40 metric tons. The payload of an airship constructed like the old Zeppelin with a length of 240 meters would amount to 130 tons.

An airship of our production series No. 2 is currently

operating in Tokyo as an airborne laboratory for echo-sounder and air-pollution measurements. This airship has a diameter of 17.5 m. The first airship built by our plant was tested in 3,000 hours of flight, and in wind velocities up to 120 knots. This experimental airship operated all year-round in ice, rain, and snow, and has not once been sent back to the hangar for repairs or technical modifications.

At our plant, we use a new hangar construction, consisting of a steel frame covered by an air-supported skin. One side of the inflatable hangar is equipped with an opening mechanism to allow the the airship to be moved in and out.

The material for the envelope of the airship is high-tenacity polyester Trevira, rubberized with a synthetic. The tenacity of this material is forty or fifty times higher than that required by law. The envelope consists of approximately 600 pieces, which are stitched together and welded. The nose-cap of the airship is reinforced with an aluminium frame. Two comparatively low-powered, standard-aircraft engines, each with a capacity of 400 hp, are attached to the gondolas, which vary in size. The engines are suspended from the gondolas by struts.

The bottom of the gondola is of steel. The rudders are made of aluminium and their thirty square meters of surface are covered with synthetic fabric. The construction of our airship is not complicated and does not require highly sophisticated technology.

Technical Specifications of the Prototype
Payload: 40 metric tons
Range: 20 hours of flight time or 40,000 km
Production Cost: US$3 million

In addition to the conventional means of transportation, the prototype could be used for distances up to a 1000 km. It could, after some technical modifications, be used as a coast-to-coast vessel in South America or as a means of transportation from agricultural or manufacturing centers to the assembly and shipping (loading) centers such as harbors. The prototype will carry up to 200 passengers; it can be used as an airborne ambulance or hospital in times of emergencies and natural disaster, because no airstrip is needed—it can take off vertically or horizontally. It is an efficient and reliable conveyance offering a large range of operating possibilities: transportation of goods and passengers, rescue operations, airborne hospital, and laboratory for echo-sounder and air-pollution measurements.

Plant and Installations Necessary for the Production of Airships

The portable hangar is spread on a level surface and inflated with air. The hangar has a length of 85 m, and a width and a height of 36 m each. It is so far the world's largest air-supported hall. Superchargers inflate the hall with air, to a total amount of 162,000 cubic meters. Two small superchargers stabilize the air pressure in the hangar. The inside barometric pressure measures 40 mm, thus enabling the hall to tolerate wind velocities up to 120 miles per hour.

An airship needs an airstrip only about twice its own length for horizontal takeoff, in contrast to the long runways required for airplanes. The construction of the gondolas allows variation in size because it does not depend on aerodynamics and solidity. Engines are attached to both sides of the gondola, and produce a speed of approximately 150 km per hour, with a noise level of 35 decibels. During flight the airship glides through the air without producing any outside noise. The amount of horsepower used for engines on larger airships is not substantially increased; we use 400-hp Rolls Royce engines. The fuel consumption amounts to 15 liters per hour per engine. The engines have to be serviced after 3,000 hours of flight time. On the ground the airship's nose-cap is tied to the mooring-mast.

The airship's vertical takeoff is effected by deflating one of the three air-filled ballons; when the ship is airborne, the engines are activated to move it forward. The normal takeoff is dynamic, for which the airship needs an airstrip only about 120

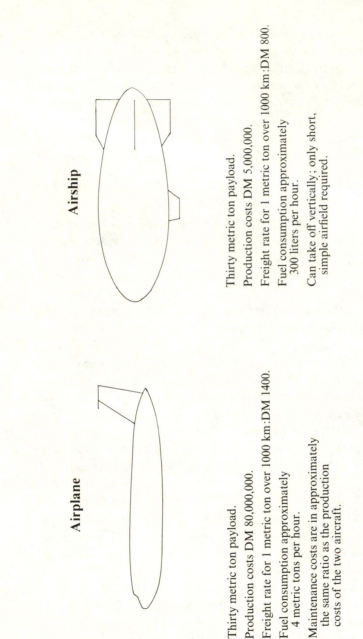

Airplane

Thirty metric ton payload.

Production costs DM 80,000,000.

Freight rate for 1 metric ton over 1000 km : DM 1400.

Fuel consumption approximately 4 metric tons per hour.

Maintenance costs are in approximately the same ratio as the production costs of the two aircraft.

Airship

Thirty metric ton payload.

Production costs DM 5,000,000.

Freight rate for 1 metric ton over 1000 km : DM 800.

Fuel consumption approximately 300 liters per hour.

Can take off vertically; only short, simple airfield required.

Fig. 52. Economic comparisons of airplane and airship

meters long. The airship can also take off and land practically everywhere without any difficulty—on meadows, fields, or football grounds. This opens a wide range of possibilities; for example, fruit or other agricultural products can be transported directly from the orchard or farm to the centers of shipping and loading. (Fig. 52)

The Contributors

MANUEL S. ALBA is director of the East-West Technology and Development Institute, East-West Center, Honolulu.

DAVID ARADEON is professor of architecture, Faculty of Environmental Design, University of Lagos, Nigeria.

GWEN BELL is editor *Ekistics* and consultant on planning human settlements.

JOSÉ CONRADO BENITEZ is program director of the Commission on Human Settlements, Development Academy of the Philippines.

GERARD BLACHÈRE is professor of architectural industrial techniques at the Conservatoire national des Arts et Métiers, Paris, France.

FREDRICH BURIAN is a documentation specialist at the Technology and Development Institute, East-West Center, Honolulu.

ERIC CARLSON is head, Human Settlements Program of the UN Environment Program, and senior program officer of the UN Habitat and Human Settlements Foundation.

GEORGE L. CHAN is a waste digester specialist with the South Pacific Commission, Noumea, New Caledonia.

ALBERT G. H. DIETZ is professor of building engineering, Massachusetts Institute of Technology.

R. BUCKMINSTER FULLER, inventor, is professor, Southern Illinois University, and World Fellow in Residence, University of Pennsylvania, Bryn Mawr College, Haverford College, Swarthmore College, and University City Science Center.

ALEJANDRO GOICOECHEA OMAR is the developer of the Talgo train that has been adopted by the Spanish railway system (RENFE).

LOUIS J. GOODMAN is assistant director for education and professional development of the East-West Technology and Development Institute, East-West Center, Honolulu.

FREDERICK GUTHEIM is professor at George Washington University and Senior Fellow at the Washington Center for Metropolitan Studies.

APRODICIO LAQUIAN is associate director for social sciences and human resources of the International Development Research Centre, Ottawa, Canada.

CARL LINDSTROM, a civil engineer specializing in sanitation and ecology, is head of the section on purification techniques of the National Swedish Environment Board.

C. A. MORRISON teaches applied thermodynamics and is director of the solar test house and calorimeter operation, University of Florida, Gainesville.

ALVARO ORTEGA is professor of architecture, McGill University, Montreal, Canada.

HASAN POERBO is professor of architecture, Bandung Institute of Technology, Indonesia.

TAYLOR A. PRYOR, marine biologist and agricultural economist, is president of the Pryor Corporation, which has developed Systemculture.

HERMANN RUHLE, engineer, is professor and deputy director, Academy of Building and Institute of Housing and Social Building, German Democratic Republic, Berlin.

BALWANT SINGH SAINI is head, Department of Architecture, University of Queensland, Australia.

E. F. SCHUMACHER, economist, is founder and chairman of the Intermediate Technology Development Group, Ltd.

GEOFFREY STANFORD is the developer of Agro-city, Greenhills, Duncanville, Texas.

ERNEST WEISSMAN, architect and town-planner, is senior consultant on regional development to the United Nations Center for Housing Building and Planning, and to the United Nations Environment Program.

THEODOR WUELLENKEMPER, pilot and flight instructor, is founder-owner of Westdeutsche Luftwerbung, which specializes in constructing airships.

BENJAMIN ZUR is director, Soils and Fertilizers Laboratory, Technion-Israel Institute of Technology, Haifa, Israel.